Gentle
Persuasion

Gentle Persuasion

Creative ways to introduce
your friends to Christ.

Joseph C. Aldrich

MULTNOMAH

Portland, Oregon 97266

Scripture references are from the Holy Bible: New International Version, copyright 1973, 1978, 1984, by the International Bible Society. Used by permission of Zondervan Bible Publishers.

Edited by Steve Halliday
Cover design and illustrations by Bruce DeRoos

GENTLE PERSUASION
© 1988 Multnomah Press
Portland, Oregon 97266

Printed in the United States of America

Library of Congress Cataloging-in-Publication Data

Aldrich, Joseph C., 1940-
   Gentle persuasion : creative ways to introduce your friends to Christ / Joseph C. Aldrich.
     p. cm.
   ISBN 0-88070-253-2 (pbk.)
   1. Witness bearing (Christianity) 2. Evangelistic work.
I. Title.
BV4520.A45 1988
248'.5—dc19   88-19828
                                            CIP

92 93 94 95 – 10 9 8 7 6 5

Contents

Genuine caring is hard to resist.

LOVE THEM 'TIL THEY ASK YOU WHY

Rumor has it that the one who ends up with the most toys wins. Pile up enough things, deep-six all competition, network the movers and shakers . . . and power, position, and status are yours to enjoy. So goes the tale.

It's a rumor, folks.

More often than not, "upward mobility" is a downer. No amount of this world's bicarbonates can ease eternal heartaches.

People need the Lord!

In fact, some of *your* people need the Lord—those who pump your gas, cut your hair, live next door, work at the next desk. God is asking you to "reach out and touch someone!"

Oh oh! What's that noise? It sounds like groaning!

"But I'm not *gifted* for evangelism," you say. "I've *tried* to use the popular methods. They don't work for me. They just don't fit. If you're planning on telling me I can get to like them, don't bother. I've tried—honestly, I have—and I've fallen flat on my face. What can you say that will make a difference?"

You'll be delighted to know that we won't be talking about "the same song, second verse" approaches to evangelism. We'll be talking about touching people in ways appropriate to your own giftedness. As I read the Scriptures, I'm haunted by the idea that God is not so much asking you to tell your people what a friend they have in Jesus, as in showing them what a friend they have in you.

Love them, we're told. Love them until they ask us why.

I recently met a fascinating, radiant Christian from India. His ministry to international students is leading scores of Hindus and Moslems to Christ. What accounts for his effectiveness in reaching members of these radically different cultural and religious traditions?

Each Sunday, he told me, he and his wife host somewhere between thirty and fifty students for dinner. That's a key part of his strategy. Food and camaraderie break down barriers. There's something about eating a meal with someone that accelerates friendship.

"So you talk about Christ at these meals?" I asked.

"No," he said. "It is impossible to talk openly of Jesus Christ."

"So how," I asked him, "are you able to see so many find Christ?"

"I love them," he replied, "until they ask me why."

His reply has a familiar ring to it. Didn't our Lord say something about loving our neighbors? Not evangelizing them, mind you, but *loving* them. In fact, nowhere in Scripture are we told to *evangelize* our neighbors.

But my Indian friend's story wasn't over.

"Through loving them," he continued, "they meet Jesus Christ, even though they don't know whom they've met. Once they've sensed the reality of his love through me, they're open to discuss the reason for the love and acceptance they've experienced."

Interesting.

Could a well-cooked meal sprinkled with lots of love start a people-flow toward the Cross?

Can you bake a cherry pie?

Part of preparing to become a redemptive person is growing in your understanding of how God draws people to himself.

If you and I were neighbors committed to reaching our cul-de-sacs for Christ, what would we do? If we were committed to seeing our fellow employees come into God's family, where would we start? What plan would we follow, what tools would we use?

"The Bible?"

I can't argue with that. It's an essential tool. But I'm also talking about using your hammer and saw, your vise-grips and your level.

"For evangelism?"

Absolutely! I'm talking about reaching folks through a well-cooked meal, a listening ear, a serving heart.

"Sounds like liberalism to me. We're called lights, not cooks! Frankly, I don't see what being a 'light' has to do with baking a cherry pie."

Now, don't be too hard on cherry pies! When we get around to looking at Isaiah 58, some new "light" may be shed on your understanding of light. But that's for later.

"Well, you're right about one thing. People need the Lord, and 'my people,' as you call them, need him, too. To be honest, I could use some help. Please understand, though, that I'm a greenhorn—and a wee bit nervous about the whole thing."

That's OK. It's perfectly natural, and perfectly fixable. Perhaps you can identify with Denise and John and their desire to see lost men and women find Jesus.

SCENE ONE: A modern-day couple confronts the evangelism scene.

Setting: *John and Denise have just returned home from*

*an evening of evangelism training. They feel challenged . . .
and guilty. Mostly, they feel discouraged and dejected. After
a few moments of tense silence, Denise speaks.*

"I just can't do it, John. I'm sorry, but I'm not
comfortable sharing with strangers."

"But Denise, you signed up for Tuesday evening!
Why didn't you speak up?"

"What could I say? 'Excuse me, please. I'm dropping
out. I'm not interested in seeing folks go to heaven.'
I *do* want to get involved in sharing my faith, but
I'm no good with words. Nothing comes out right."

"Denise, that was the whole point of the evening—
to teach us what to say and how to say it. We all
need help, dear."

"I know, John, but . . . I'm uneasy about it. Seems
to me it's such a narrow, such a limited strategy. It
doesn't fit me."

"Well, I wish you'd spoken up sooner. We're committed now."

"I know, I know. But what could I have said? Who
wants to oppose evangelism? Let's drop it. You just
don't understand."

Research indicates that only about 10 percent of believers are gifted to share Christ using the methods presented
in almost 100 percent of the classes on personal
evangelism. My concern is to give those 10 percent 100
percent of my support, while unleashing the other 90
percent to discover and fulfill their critical role in the
evangelism process.

A major people-flow into our local churches is not
likely until the majority function as fully redemptive

people—people who use their gifts and abilities for re-demptive purposes.

What you feel about evangelism is probably not new. It's always been tough and a bit unnerving. You're not alone.

SCENE TWO: Amos and Zechariah, two ordinary, unremarkable, first-century followers of Jesus, are about to become Christian witnesses.

Setting: *Almost twenty centuries ago, seventy-plus folks were being trained by Jesus of Nazareth to evangelize the towns and villages of their world.*

Amos and Zechariah were scared spitless (Scripture doesn't give us the names of any of the seventy-two, but we'll imagine Amos and Zach were among them). Tagged by the Lord for his next big soul-saving campaign, they had the pre-trip jitters. The newly drafted evangelists had had no quarrel with the Master's decision to ship out the "Big Twelve" to pioneer saving the world—that was *his* business. All reports indicated that their efforts had been moderately successful. But those guys were super-heavyweights, with a capital "S"! We're talking first string, varsity. Especially Peter, James, and John. They could preach and teach and mash mental machinery with the best of them.

But Amos and Zach? They felt very ordinary and in-adequate. They were one-syllable, one-cylinder type of guys—bench warmers, if you please. When it came to helping Jesus, passing out bulletins and sweeping synagogues was more their style. They'd even clip coupons, push grocery carts, and dry the dishes if it'd make life a little easier for their friend. But that wasn't what the Lord had in mind.

Jesus said he was going to use *them* in evangelism.

Quick! What to do? Could they torch the draft cards, defect, flunk boot camp? No, that wouldn't work. They remembered an ancient relative's three-day cruise in the steaming guts of a Nineveh-bound whale, and they admitted that God's call was irrevocable.

So what's a man to do? They stood with seventy other reluctant draftees, togas trembling, knees knocking, listening hard to the details of their upcoming foray. They all agreed with the mission statement: Those without Christ were going to hell. Period.

The unsolved mystery was how Jesus could possibly use underdogs like them. Surely he must know something they didn't! Is it any wonder they hung on every word? They'd been around long enough to know that poor folks (like them) need to take rich folks out to dinner and listen, because success leaves clues.

Hadn't Jesus coached the varsity boys to a winning season? His strategy had paid off. There was no doubt the coach was rich in experience, courage, and confidence.

It was a good thing. His rag-tag second team needed more than a little of each. Random thoughts secretly tested and challenged the Lord's instructions. Perhaps you will recognize some of them.

"You're serious, Lord? You're really serious? You *are* serious!"

"Us, Lord? You've got plans for Amos and me? You're kidding."

"Lord, I can fix a boat, repair a chariot, fix a leaky faucet, bake a cherry pie—but I'm not into evangelism."

"Why don't you stick with the world-class pros? This isn't a job for lay folks."

"It's tax season."

"I've never felt comfortable talking about God and stuff."

"I'm a homebody—not the traveling type."

"Wouldn't ads in the local paper be more effective?"

"Why isn't Jesus going with us?"

"Nobody's interested in God and hell and eternity."

"I don't want to make a fool of myself. I'm a respected person in my community!"

"Isn't there some other way?"

"Jesus sounds narrow to me. Why not let folks worship the way they want to?"

"I don't want to eat and sleep with strangers!"

"We've got more than enough priests and Levites running around already. Why couldn't the Lord use some of them?"

"How about a crusade evangelist?"

"You don't know my wife, Lord; she'd never stand for it."

"I've got teenagers. The last thing they need is for dad to become a Jesus freak."

"Here am I, Lord; *SEND HIM!*"

They never dreamed that God Almighty would inspire Luke's pen to jot down their soul-saving exploits in Holy Writ. Luke tells us that the Lord split up the seventy-two and sent them out. Spiritual training wheels in place, thirty-six rag-tag teams ventured out to extend the kingdom of light over the kingdom of darkness.

How did they do? Luke 10:17 records that they proclaimed the gospel and "returned with joy."

You know what? So can you!

You can reach your cul-de-sac for Christ!

Don't get me wrong. It's a long, hard road from fear to joy. Fortunately, there are some signposts along the way. Some of them are tucked away in Luke's heartwarming account of the sending of the seventy.* We'll stop at regular intervals to take a look at the signs, and to be encouraged that we, too, can be used to bring people to Christ. Some ideas will come up more than once; use their multiple appearances to fix in your mind an effective strategy appropriate to your own gifts and interests.

Plugging in where God has gifted us to fit is what it's all about. Isn't it about time we got back to the Bible's way of moving people toward the Christ of the Cross?

* (We'll refer to this group as "the seventy," even though it was comprised of seventy-two men.)

Learn to use your talents winsomely.

1

Ｉf you aim at nothing, you'll hit it every time.

Evangelism is no exception. Not having a goal won't ad-

CAN YOU BAKE A CHERRY PIE?

vance the cause of Christ. But even having a goal doesn't ensure success. It's equally futile to have a goal without developing a strategy to reach it.

Mark it down: To be an effective, redemptive person, you must have both a goal and a strategy.

A Working Definition of Strategy

The dictionary tells us that strategy involves "skillful management in getting the better of an adversary or attaining an end." Notice three important parts of the definition. First, a strategy demands skillful management to attain an "end." An "end" is an old-fashioned word for a goal or objective. You can have a goal (to reach your neighbors) without a strategy, but you can't have a strategy without a goal.

Second, it takes "skillful management" to reach a goal. Even in evangelism! Soulcraft is most effective when people know what they want to accomplish and then carry out a plan necessary to achieve it. The cultivatior.

of a soul is often a much longer and more difficult challenge than most of us think. It takes diligence, courage, and faith in about equal amounts.

Third, most "goals" have to be reached by overcoming specific obstacles. The obstacles of a busy schedule, conflicting priorities, and cultural barriers quickly come to mind. For every action, it seems, there is an equal and opposite reaction. Count on it, friend, everything that is good will be opposed. To reach a lost friend, we must "get the better of an adversary." The enemy, by the way, is not that non-Christian friend—he's a victim of the enemy. The Bible calls Satan the ultimate adversary.

"So what do I do?" you ask. "Quite honestly, I don't have a clue. Are you saying I need a strategy?"

You're definitely on the right track. Evangelism isn't throwing hamburger in a fan and hoping someone opens his mouth. What we do is largely determined by what we think.

One of the best places to get our thinking straight is to look into Luke's Gospel for some traces of our Lord's strategy. There we can see how the master Teacher prepared the seventy for ministry. Let's roost awhile on four ideas.

Look at some key phrases from Luke 10:1. Underline "*After this,*" "*the Lord appointed,*" "*sent them two by two,*" and "*to every town and place where he was about to go.*" Let's take them one by one.

After this:
Becoming a redemptive person involves preparation

It's no accident that "*After this*" begins verse one of chapter ten. "After this" forces us to ask "after what?" We can't understand the effectiveness of Mission Seventy without taking a hike through the previous context. That's what Luke wants us to do. A trip through chapter nine helps us see the preparation which preceded the sending of the seventy. How do you think each of these experiences prepared the seventy for their mission?

Jesus sends out the twelve, 9:1-6

Herod the tetrarch is perplexed by the results of this mission, 9:7-9

Jesus feeds the five thousand, 9:10-17

Peter's confession of Christ, 9:18-21

Jesus reveals his death, 9:22

Jesus reveals the high cost of discipleship, 9:23-27, 57-62

Jesus is transfigured, 9:28-36

Jesus heals a demon-possessed boy, 9:37-45

The disciples argue about who will be the greatest, 9:46-50

Opposition from the Samaritans, 9:51-56

Note carefully that the "curriculum" for the seventy grew out of life itself. What they saw, felt, and experienced of Christ was supremely important. They didn't get appointed to the Mission Seventy task force because of their academic or social credentials. The critical qualification seems to be that they followed Jesus. It was their relationship to the Savior which mattered, not the number of badges pinned to their lapels. Few, if any, were seminarians or theologs. Those kind aren't usually very effective in evangelism anyway. They're too cerebral. And most folks aren't argued into the kingdom.

The fact is, *your relationship to Christ is the single most*

important qualification for becoming a redemptive person.
Your experience of Christ is the cornerstone of your preparation for ministry. A witness is a witness . . . to something. A witness talks about what he has seen, felt, and
experienced. He communicates the reality of Christ's
presence in the brokenness of his life. He communicates
from the platform of his victories and defeats, his joys
and sorrows. It's pretty difficult to communicate what
you haven't experienced.

Witnessing involves describing such things as:

How Christ changed your marriage.

How Christ altered your vocabulary.

How peace has become a reality in your life.

How God's forgiveness brings joy.

How a new sense of purpose and meaning fills your
life.

How you are increasingly being delivered from frus-
trating and sometimes destructive habits.

Please note that most of these items can be *demon-
strated* as well as *declared*. Evangelism is both *show* and
tell. More about that later.

Let's get back to the seventy. What pivotal events
helped prepare them for their evangelism assignment?
Let's look at a few of those events, and see if we can pick
up a few pointers.

**1. Before the Lord deployed the seventy, he did a
test-run with the twelve.**

The apostles were the guinea pigs. Jesus sent them out
alone. The Lord stayed home. They soloed. Don't miss
how significant that is!

Before they left, Christ endowed them with the authority to heal the sick and cast out demons. He gave them the ability to do what they'd observed him doing. Now it was their turn. Now they were the performers, representing their Lord.

These newly-appointed ambassadors hitched up their pants, tightened their sandals, took a deep breath, and marched out and did it. Elbows swinging, they scattered, preaching and healing folks from city hall to the farmer's market. Eureka! They did what he did! They spoke the word, and it happened. Bones mended, sickness disappeared, demons were cratered. It worked! Folks were impressed. Jesus, of course, wasn't with them—but make no mistake, he *was* with them. That's why it worked.

That's still why it works. Jesus is with us. We are co-laborers with him. Do we believe that? We're not prepared if we don't. Sheep among wolves won't last long if they try to take on the fanged crowd by themselves.

Why did the Lord leave his disciples on their own? It was necessary for them to learn he would "never leave them or forsake them." The impact of the Lord working through the twelve was thrilling, awesome. As you might imagine, the news of their exploits spread like honey on a hot rock.

"Hey, Zechariah! You healed anyone lately?"

"Who, me?"

"Yea, buddy, you. Have you prayed and seen cripples walk and the blind start seeing and stuff like that?"

"Come on, John, don't hand me that. What on God's green earth are you raving about?"

"Well, since you brought it up: A dozen or so of us boys got sent out by Jesus to help him out a bit. You know, to pray for folks and teach them about

God. The Lord told us to drive out some demons and cure some diseases. I suppose I saw a dozen or so crippled up people get straightened out. Don't mention it, of course; we don't want to stir up much of a commotion."

"My lips are sealed."

And if you believe his lips were sealed . . . I know a famous bridge on special this weekend. But back to that first missionary journey.

Imagine the impact when they returned from the towns and villages and started describing their incredible experiences! Is it any wonder they got involved in a debate over who was the greatest? The party lines were humming. As story upon story overloaded the rumor circuits, the seventy got the message. Joy was bouncing around. People were doing backflips up and down the sidewalks. Chances are, some of the relatives of the seventy were cured. Others repented and were saved. Certainly, everyone began to understand what it meant to be co-laborers with God.

2. The return of the twelve motivated the seventy.

God not only stretched his first-stringers, he let their successes and failures encourage and challenge the "phase two" folks. Nothing succeeds like success. But the ripples didn't stop with the seventy. In fact, the unprecedented outpouring of power sent shock waves right past the seventy and shook the throne room of Herod himself. That old fox thought the game was over when he'd lifted the head of John the Baptist. Boy, was he wrong.

Certainly part of good preparation is to know that others have succeeded. I guess we all have a little bit of "anything you can do, I can do better" in us. Let's face it, success breeds success. It was true in those days, it's true today.

"God," shouted Mike, "If you'll let my kid score a touchdown, I'll be in church next Sunday."

He was serious, and a wee bit desperate. His son's team was scoreless in six games, and it seemed God was their only hope. Mike's frustration was boiling over. Sometimes the only option play left is prayer.

Would you believe, my friend, that on the very next play, Mike's son was given the ball, a hole opened up in the line, and the boy ran sixty yards for a touchdown? The first touchdown, mind you, in *six* games. Don't tell me God doesn't play football! The scoreless drought was over. The crowd roared its approval.

When the celebrating subsided, Mike's buddies in the stands reminded him of his oath. They weren't about to let him off the hook.

"So, Saint Mike, you'll be in church next Sunday? Right?"

"I'll be there," Mike promised.

That possibility may have been a greater miracle than the sixty-yard touchdown run. Mike, by the way, had no problem choosing a church. The man sitting next to him was not only his friend and the father of another boy on the team, he was pastor of a local congregation. True to his word, Mike showed up for church. True to his Word, God answered the pastor's prayers and Mike came forward and committed his life to Christ. Two weeks later his son received Christ.

About six weeks later I had the opportunity to meet this new brother. His conversion fired me up again about reaching the lost and confirmed some fundamental biblical principles.

Mike's prayer of desperation was no accident. Nor was the hole in the line or the sixty-yard touchdown caper. God was in the huddle, God was in the stands. It was no accident that Mike and the pastor became friends. In fact, Mike's new birth was the result of that pastor's deliberate strategy of infiltration and cultivation.

You could do that! Knowing that the gospel flows down webs of relationships, the pastor chose to network with all the folks associated with the team. This included parents, players, and coaches. He supported his son, he supported the team, he supported its extended family. You could do that too!

With prayerful expectancy, this man positioned himself within a key web of relationships and waited for God to open doors—or, in this case, a hole in the line so a frustrated father could find life in Christ. It makes sense.

Co-laborers work together, sharing resources. God plus you plus an unsaved friend is a dynamite combination. But there's no sense preparing if we don't expect results. You've heard it: "Woe, it's the last days! Oh, the apostasy! Nobody's interested! Alas!" and all that stuff. If we could just get our pastor to pound a little harder and shout a little louder!

"You don't understand, Joe, I'm just a worm. Just a lil', insignificant worm crawling around in the dust."

Friend, what you "see" is usually what you get. Go bite an apple! The tragedy is that the average Christian has no non- Christian friends after he's known the Lord for two years. We limit our fishing to the stained glass aquarium. We've been deceived by the wolf pack.

"Hold it! Hold it right there, brother Aldrich. Mike was reached by one of the pros. A pastor, no less. A cemetery graduate, if you will. I'm just an ordinary Amos.

I thought this book was for ordinary people!"

Good point. You're more perceptive than I hoped you'd be! But I'm glad you asked.

Actually, a pastor has a lot more handicaps than advantages when it comes to being a redemptive neighbor. It's true he probably knows more than most. But I'll bet you'd rather tell a new acquaintance that you're an "Independent Agent" than "Pastor of the Independent Baptist Church." A reverend next door isn't usually a pagan's idea of a good neighbor. Believe me, I know what I'm talking about. When I was in the pastorate, I told them I was in the counseling business.

"I guess I'd never thought of it that way. OK, I'm still with you. You were talking about strategy from Luke . . ."

Chapter ten. The first verse. We were looking at what happened before "After this."

3. Before the Lord sent out the seventy, he fed five thousand folks fish and chips from a little guy's lunch sack.

That sack sensation not only made the evening news, it blew the socks off all the local Houdinis. What an incredible, unforgettable visual aid! It's entirely possible that most of the seventy saw the lad's meal multiply. This Jesus was no mere man!

It's pretty hard to deny tangible evidence of the supernatural when you're touching, smelling, and swallowing wonder bread. Those supernatural crusts even softened up some who were still suffering from hardening of the categories. There was nothing fishy about the fish, either. Real fish. Hundreds of them. From one lunch sack! Five thousand satisfied customers spread the word.

The bus boys featured at this memorable potluck were the "dazzlin' dozen." The insiders. Hadn't they just returned from their own "miracle tour?" It was one time in their lives they didn't mind being waiters. You can almost hear them talk:

> "Yea, you're right. I can see how you guys probably think feeding all these folks from a kid's lunch is a big deal. Believe me, it's no big thing. Really! Take it from me—you wouldn't believe the heavy-duty stuff he does when we're alone with him. You know, just us apostles and him. It's awesome, just awesome."

They were prouder than peacocks in full bloom.

They were also showboatin' phonies.

Though they'd eaten fish and chips, these men had egg on their faces. Perhaps the greatest lesson to be gained from the feeding of the five thousand is what it revealed about the "dazzlin' dozen" (and us!). The master Teacher followed up dinner with a little "pop quiz" for his inflated waiters. A bath in the freezing brine of a raging sea brought things into focus for them. After the Lord let them churn about for a time, he showed up strolling up and down the waves . . . without a surfboard! Peter's aborted water walk was a nice finishing touch to a memorable evening.

4. The Lord challenged and tested their faith.

Let's back up a bit. That morning, news had come to Jesus about the death of his cousin, John the Baptist. Grieved, he climbed in a borrowed boat and rowed off to be by himself. But the crowds found him; they always do. They brought their sick, their lame, the diseased, crippled, and fevered. All of them bounced and flailed their way toward that solitary figure. Their families clamored for his attention.

He had compassion on them and kept healing them right through lunch and dinner. Finally, the disciples had had enough. "This is a remote place, and it's already getting late," they said. "Send the crowds away. You've healed enough of them. What more do they expect?"

The Lord threw the ball back into their court: "They don't need to go away. You give them something to eat."

The disciples counted their change and realized they were a day late and a dollar short. Again they suggested he send the crowd home. But that's not what he did. Remember what happened?

The Lord had them all sit down, and in front of everyone he took the lad's lunch and said a prayer. From a rational perspective it was ludicrous. Here's a man inviting thousands of hungry people to join him for dinner from a young boy's lunch sack. But it happened!

Twenty centuries later, he comes to you and me and says: "Your neighbors and friends are spiritually malnourished. They need the Bread of Life. Don't send them away. Give them something to eat."

It seems to me that we must ask ourselves two questions. Do we care about people? Do we believe Jesus? A "yes" answer to both is an important start in preparing to become redemptive people. But like the lad, we've got to give him our all before he's apt to multiply it.

The bottom line is this: Without Jesus, the five thousand would have gone home hungry.

Without Jesus, your friends and relatives are going to hell.

"Whew! You're really smoking."

I suppose you're right. I don't understand all I know. But if language means anything, then those without Christ face an eternity in hell, an eternal existence devoid of everything that is right and pure and beautiful and light.

"And good and wholesome."

Right. Won't be any friends in hell. No buddies. No parties. Only hatred, mistrust, remorse, pain, emptiness. And loneliness! Imagine the horror of being cut off from all that satisfies, from all that fulfills and is meaningful. The restraining ministry of the Spirit will be gone.

"All hell will break loose?"

All hell will break loose. There will be no restraining of greed, lust, selfishness, and hate. *Never!* The reality is that God gives people what they choose.

"I guess I'd never thought of it that way."

If a person chooses to reject Jesus, who is goodness, love, and truth personified, he chooses to separate himself from the only one who can provide an eternal, abundant life. Hell is a perfect term for the opposite of all that Jesus is and what He stands for.

"Do you think it's part of Satan's strategy to dull our sense of lostness? You know, to make us really doubt what the Bible says about eternal . . . how shall I say it . . . damnation?"

If my experience means anything, I'd have to say "yes." When the Word prevails in my thinking, the lostness of man is overwhelming. Part of good preparation is to take seriously what God says about the lostness of man. In the long run, no one else's opinion really matters.

The one who fed the five thousand is this world's only Bread of Life. He is not content to be holed up in a lad's lunch sack, or hidden under a bushel basket. He wants to be displayed like a city on a hill. You can't miss a city on a hill. It's visible day or night.

At this point in Luke's Gospel, Jesus is soon to be

crucified. He's preparing his followers to represent him when he's gone. They must go in his name and by faith unleash the power and love of God in their world. The Bread of Life must again be offered to the multitudes so that they, too, may "taste and see that the Lord is good."

5. Before the Lord deployed the seventy, he introduced a revolutionary communication strategy.

The disciples didn't know it, but they were soon to become members of the "second incarnation." When Jesus left the earth, they were commissioned to "make visible the invisible God" in the same way Christ did. The twelve healed, cast out demons, and preached "in his name" as his representatives. They were to do as he did, speak as he spoke, love as he loved, live as he lived. In a very real sense, they became his legs and arms and heart.

Now Jesus has passed the commission to us. To share the bread, we've got to live the life.

A Christian attorney is not simply an attorney; he's God's representative in the courtroom to show the judge and jury what God is like when he tries a court case.

A Christian secretary is not simply a secretary; she's God's representative in the typing pool to demonstrate what God is like when He takes dictation, or types a letter.

A mature Christian homemaker isn't simply a mother and maid. Those hands that soothe a fevered brow demonstrate how God responds to sickness and sorrow, pressure and pain.

When folks come and ask us "the reason for the hope that is in us," they ought to see Christ in us, the hope of glory. They ought to see a radical, caring response to the pain and suffering common to man. That's why you're often most powerful for God when the pain is at its worst.

"Are you saying that evangelism is a way of living?"

You bet! Evangelism is a way of revealing the universals of God's character through the particulars of everyday living. It involves talking and living.

"Whoa! What does that mean?"

Sorry. Evangelism is godliness fleshed out. The Word became flesh. Jesus pitched his tent among us for over thirty years so we could see the Light. I suppose Jesus could have accomplished his redemptive mission by being on earth for three or four days, yet he lived among us for more than thirty years.

"Oh, I get what you're saying. Didn't he say that 'if you've seen me, you've seen the father'? "

Exactly. Furthermore, he came to "make visible the invisible God."

"I think I'm getting it. Jesus was the Light of the world. Right? So what do people see when they 'see the light'? "

A very perceptive question! According to John, the Lord's *life* was the Light of the world. Does that help?

"'His life was the Light'—the way he lived 'spoke.' But certainly, he spoke, too! I'll have to think about that. And now we are the lights of the world, and you say we become lights when his life is revealed through us. That sort of makes us the message, doesn't it?"

Couldn't have said it better myself!

6. Before the Lord sent out the seventy, he revealed his glory to Peter, James, and John.

"We have seen his glory," John wrote, "the glory of the one and only Son, who came from the Father, full of grace and truth" (John 1:14). Matthew tells us that when the Father spoke on that glory-filled mountain, Peter, James, and John "fell facedown to the ground, terrified" (Matthew 17:6). Isaiah did the same thing when he got a glimpse of God's glory: "Woe to me! I am ruined! For I am a man of unclean lips . . ." (Isaiah 6:5). Cleansed by a coal from the altar, Isaiah arose and said, "Here am I. Send me!" (Isaiah 6:8).

There's something about God's glory that brings things into focus. Values change. Priorities are rearranged. Energies are redirected.

Glory is nothing to mess around with. Only God has the real thing; all other glories are derived from him. To distort, cover, or ignore his glory is tragic. Israel blew it on this very count.

At Horeb they made a calf and worshiped an idol cast from metal. They exchanged their Glory for an image of a bull, which eats grass (Psalm 106:19-20).

"God?" the Israelites asked. "Don't worry about him. He's out there in the pasture somewhere. Toss him a bale of hay. He'll be OK. Let's get back to our pagan revelry." The more they did, the more they became like the image they worshiped. No longer were they a light to the nations. In fact, God divorced them because of their spiritual prostitution.

God's glory cannot be ignored with impunity. To replace it with a lesser glory is spiritual adultery. His glory is the fundamental reality. It is the magnetic North Pole of the moral universe. All goals, all choices, all directions must be determined by and subject to that reality.

A key step in preparing to become a redemptive person is to hold up to his radiant glory all our dreams, goals, and desires. The things of earth will grow strangely dim, and that which remains we should pursue with all our energy and strength. Touched with a coal from the altar of his glory, we proclaim, "Here am I, Lord. Send me!"

In the few years of public ministry, Jesus flooded the

land with his glory. His glory was

> proclaimed at his birth,
> heard when he taught,
> seen when he loved,
> felt when he healed,
> demonstrated when he forgave,
> revealed by his life,
> invincible when he cleansed the temple,
> veiled when he walked this earth,
> mocked when he was tried,
> disgraced when he was beaten,
> ridiculed when he hung on the cross,
> buried in a borrowed tomb,
> vindicated through his resurrection.

It continues to be

> splashed across the universe of sparkling stars and spinning galaxies,
> demonstrated through the wonders of redemption,
> accentuated through every sinner who comes home,
> the ultimate reality which demands and deserves reverence from every creature.

The Lord's Transfiguration changed forever the disciples' concept of their Lord and their response to his majesty. We, too, must present ourselves as instruments of righteousness, designed for noble purposes, ready to fulfill his will on this earth. When laid before him, the meager loaves and fishes in our sack can feed thousands.

7. Before the Lord sent out the seventy, he taught them it was going to be tough.

He was right! Go with God, and there will be pain. Go without God, and (you guessed it) there will be pain. Either way, there's pain. The trick is to get the pain working for you, not against you.

Perhaps the church in America is so lethargic because we've got it too easy. Don't misunderstand: I've got a low pain threshold; I'm not asking for pain. But I've often wondered if a little pain wouldn't help. It's so easy to drift, to compromise, to be Sunday Christians.

Go with God, and there will be pressure. Some of it will come from the pit of hell, from the lair of the evil one. Is it any wonder that before Amos and Zechariah hit the trail, Luke records our Lord's encounter with a demon-possessed boy? The "dazzlin' dozen" couldn't drive the demon out. It took Jesus himself to liberate the lad.

Satan doesn't surrender territory easily. Not in your office, not in your neighborhood. Yet Jesus ripped the lad out of the demon's grasp and delivered him healed to his dad's lap. We can, Paul reminds us, "do all things through Christ who strengthens us."

I won't kid you—there's a price to be paid for being a redemptive neighbor. But there are rewards which make it worth it all. Be prepared! "He that winneth souls is wise."

Let's look now at the other three stratagems recorded by Luke.

The Lord appointed:
Becoming a redemptive person involves a decision

The Jonah escapade reminds us that it's best to stay on the good side of how things work . . . unless you're into whale bellies. Don't take a trip if God tags you. If he speaks, listen. If he calls, go. If he asks, give.

The same Lord who tagged Amos and Zechariah appointed Jonah. He told Jeremiah that he'd been chosen to be a prophet, even before his conception. And lo and behold, he was a prophet. All his life.

To each person God has given specific, tangible, concrete abilities for ministry. Like fixing cars, repairing furniture, fishing, hunting, sewing, cooking, reading, mowing lawns, waxing cars, listening, cleaning—and I suppose I should include the old traditional list of things such as exhortation, edification, administration, and expository preaching. Any ability which brings glory to God and furthers his purposes is a spiritual gift. God expects us to use them; that's why he gave them to us.

"Joe, you've backed into this obedience stuff several times. Isn't it getting sort of thick? Everything I read encourages me to assert myself. Besides, aren't 'Weekends made for Michelob'?"

You know better than that.

"Well, I suppose I do. I'm still nervous, though, about all this 'giving up my right to convenience' talk."

Does the idea bother you?

"Well, sorta. I've got a life to live, and not enough time to live it in. You know, I don't want to become a prude, or a missionary, or some kind of religious fanatic."

I understand. But stop and think. We all serve something or someone. To what kind of master do we devote our time and energy? What are the returns?

There's an even more important question. What is God's purpose for this earth, and how do you and I fit into that purpose? Isn't that the fundamental question? When we come to the end of our lives, with only death in our future, what will it take to make us satisfied? Don't we want above all else to hear him say, "well done, thou good and faithful servant"? If we do, we must respond to his call now.

We're co-laborers with God. God's plan is for every believer to become a redemptive person by exercising his unique gifts. If we'll do our part, he'll break open a scoreless season to reach a dad and his son. He may even use a cherry pie to open up the hearts of your friends. We fit into God's purpose by loving him, obeying him, and by loving others until they ask us why.

Remember, if the Lord appoints, the Lord provides. He never calls us to do something unless he enables us to do it. Jonah's story didn't end washed up in the sand. He went to Nineveh and preached them into the king- dom. Philip hitched a ride with an Ethiopian who just "happened" to be reading from Isaiah. The man became a Christian.

God arranged those appointments for Jonah and Philip, for Amos and Zechariah, for Mike and his son. Don't miss yours. God probably won't send a missionary from Japan to reach your web of relationships.

He sent them two by two:
Becoming a redemptive person involves accountability

Amos had the jitters, but by gum, if Zach could tough it out, so could he. Zechariah was petrified, but he wasn't going to let Amos know. The Lord appointed him, and Zach had signed on come fog or freezing rain. The two men encouraged each other to stick with it.

As iron sharpens iron, the Bible tells us, so a man sharpens his friends. Friends encourage us, challenge us, and confront us. Friends hold us accountable and pray us through to success.

When Ruthe and I were on Campus Crusade staff, we

were required to share the gospel with fifteen collegians per week. Whatever one might think of the requirement, having to fill out a weekly report kept us hopping—and that's not all bad. A friend can do the same thing. Friends become valuable resource people as they share their successes and failures.

Let's put it straight. Maturity is always a return to reality about yourself. Physical growth requires food. Mental and spiritual growth require feedback. As long as we won't face the truth, we remain in protracted infancy.

Why not consider telling a friend of your desire to become a redemptive person? Let him or her pray with you as you begin the process of finding your place in the process of evangelism and functioning according to your own giftedness.

He sent them to every town and place where he was about to go:
Becoming a redemptive person requires a sharp focus

"If you don't know where you're going, when you get there, you won't know where you are." Do you like that? I picked it up from a crusty old New Englander.

Jesus didn't send the "dazzlin' dozen" everywhere. It wasn't "every man for himself." Nor did he send them bombing through cloud cover. They were carefully focused. Jesus not only knew the troops he was sending out (that's you and me), he knew about the places they were going. He probably used an overhead and a map of the area: "OK boys, hit this town, and the one just south of it. Forget Capernaum. Why would I want to go there?" Jesus sharply focused his troops.

"So how do I find my village and unleash my stuff on

it?" you ask. "With folks all around me, can you tell me how to find the fish that will bite?"

Yes, in fact, I can tell you. But I won't. Not now, anyway. The secret is tucked away in Luke 10.

"So you're going to make me wait?"

Couldn't have said it better myself!

Notice that the mission of the seventy was to prepare each village for the coming of Jesus. In like manner, we are commissioned to prepare webs of relationships so that Jesus may come to them. That's how we labor together with the Billy Grahams of this world. We do the spade work, we build the relationships, and then God brings along someone gifted in reaping to harvest what we have cultivated and sown. It could be a pastor, an evangelist, a film, a book . . . or even you.

Wrapping It Up

Although we don't really know the names of any of the seventy, we do know their fears. We, too, fear rejection, failure, and persecution. We don't want to be weird, to seem narrow and sectarian.

It's hard for most of us to confront a scientific age with an ancient book. Standing against the drift of our culture and leaning against its prevailing wind isn't fun. Besides, this old world holds lots of appeal. It may offer rat poison disguised as bread, but it does sparkle and shine. The gusto we're going for eludes our grasp, but we're getting after it, and when we capture it, then we'll get serious about loving our neighbor and reaching our world. At one time or another, I guess we've all cycled through these same fears and temptations.

Amos and Zechariah have gone on to their reward. They served well. We live in a different time, culture, and world, but we stand accountable to the same commission.

God has his Peters, Jameses, and Johns; his Billy Grahams, Chuck Swindolls and Joni Eareckson Tadas. I thank God for such gifted people and the impact God has privileged them to make. Such godly giants are few and far between. But their ministries depend upon the faithfulness of common foot soldiers like Amos, Zechariah, you and me. Officers without an army are impotent. Billy Graham and others acknowledge that their ministries would be severely limited were it not for the troops in the trenches.

Therefore, let's unleash the foot soldiers. Turn them loose! Wouldn't you be interested in utilizing your skills, gifts, and hobbies as redemptive tools?

Suppose the biblical concept of persuasion was far broader than most of our one-dimensional evangelism models would lead us to believe? Then this book on evangelism could turn out to be *good* news for you! It advocates a biblical strategy that takes seriously your own giftedness, and doesn't expect you to exercise gifts you don't have.

Can you bake a cherry pie? How about loaning someone a lawn mower? Someone's neighbor found Christ through just such a kind gesture. I'll tell you about it later.

Proper vision is a key to success.

2

SEEING IS BELIEVING

Let it crackle, hiss, and spit. As long as the old radio populated the theater of our minds with villains and heroes, danger, romance, and lots of suspense, nobody cared. Those glowing tubes transported us to a land of adventure and thrills where imagination ruled.

Do you remember the cowboys and Indians, the war whoops and circled wagons? Can you see the attack developing? Indian war horses with ears back, nostrils flared, flanks heaving, sweep their riders toward the unsuspecting wagon train. Just before disaster strikes, the cowboys discover their peril and desperately circle the wagons. Who can forget the suspense, the war paint, the cowboy hats, the flash of flaming arrows or the deadly bark of the '94 Winchesters?

How would you imagine the scene if we changed the characters? If instead of cowboys and Indians, the enemies were the forces of hell versus you and me (the church), who would be cowering behind the circled wagons, and who would be charging on war horses? Would the troops of hell or of the church have grease paint on their cheeks? Would Christ, the head of the church, wear a Stetson or eagle feathers?

Our Chief didn't leave us to guess. He said, "I will build my church, and the gates of the fortress of hell will not be able to withstand the church's attack." No, he wouldn't be wearing a Stetson or firing a Winchester.

The church is no haven until heaven, no refuge until the Rapture. Nor is it a fortress to be defended, or the National Guard. It's an army focused *outward* whose soldiers are deployed into barber shops, gas stations, businesses, and neighborhoods where the lost live, serve, and work.

Let's change the image. What would you think of a church that pictured itself as a Spirit-filled department store, a place where all the sanitized employees show up at 7:30 A.M., march in, lock the doors, and sell Christian merchandise to each other all day? You'd probably snicker at it. Yet how far removed is that picture from the way many of us operate? Such a vision is costly to the cause of Christ.

Søren Kierkegaard, a Danish philosopher, once encountered a woman upset because a dance had been held in the church building. "What night of the week was the building used for a dance?" he asked. Informed it was a Saturday night, he replied, "It's far better to use the church on Saturday night for a dance than to use it Sunday morning to mock God."

An Imaginary Visit by Jesus

Imagine that it's Sunday morning at your church. Today Jesus has accepted an invitation to come up to the platform to be interviewed. He's there every Sunday morning, so we may as well take advantage of his presence. He usually sits near the front on the right-hand side.

"Greetings on behalf of all the membership at The

Church of the Immaculate Perception. Delighted you're with us, Lord!"

"Always good to be with my people, Joe."

"You honor us with your presence. Our time is somewhat limited this morning; we've got lots of things going, you know."

"That's true, Joe. Things seem to be hopping."

"A couple of questions, Lord. First, is it true that you are omniscient?"

"Yes, Joe, I know everything."

"Is it also true that you have commissioned us to reach the world?"

"Absolutely. You're my witnesses, my ambassadors, my 'fishers of men.'"

"Is it fair to say that we become the channels through which you touch the lives of people?"

"Oh, yes! When love is felt, the message is heard. Paul 'made himself a servant, to win as many as possible.' He loved, cared, preached, and suffered to see the lost find me."

"So, you work in and through us. In a very real sense, we become your arms, legs, mouth, and heart. People are moved toward the Cross as we flow into their lives to love, serve, and communicate the gospel."

"Exactly. You're now the lights of the world. It's your turn to reach out and touch someone. Of course, I'm with you."

"All right, Lord. These folks in the audience are about to leave this service. As I understand it, they're supposed to represent you in offices, parking lots, stores, and neighborhoods all over town. Is that correct?"

"Yes, Joe."

"You, of course, already know whether you will have

significant, redemptive contact through the arms, legs, mouths, and hearts of these, your people. You already know what's going to happen this week."

"That's right."

"Are you looking forward to your week?"

"Well . . . no. No, I'm not."

A gasp whips through the congregation. Startled listeners snap awake to see tears coursing down the cheeks of their Master. *No? What does he mean, 'no'?* they whisper to each other.

Head down, speech laced with sorrow, Jesus continues:

"No, I'll have no significant, redemptive contact this week through the lives of these people. They're going out expecting nothing, and that's what they'll get. They have no vision."

Then he'd leave.

You know, it really is far better to use the church for a dance Saturday night than to use it to mock God Sunday morning. We're not to wait for the Indians to find the circled wagons, lay down their arms, and come join us behind the wheels. We're not called to do our fishing in the stained glass aquarium. Our vision must be outward bound. "When the saints go marching out" is what we sing.

Successful Evangelism Is Vision-Driven

Notice what the Lord told Amos, Zechariah, and their buddies:

> *The harvest is plentiful, but the workers are few. Ask the Lord of the harvest, therefore, to send out workers into his harvest field* (Luke 10:2).

In a gospel that records only 151 words of our Lord's instruction—about seventy seconds worth—why the reference to an abundant crop and a labor shortage? It's my conviction that the Spirit directed Luke to record those critical parts of our Lord's teaching which would someday impact readers in Portland, Oregon, and Portland, Maine, and all stops in between.

Isn't it interesting that the first words Jesus speaks to the seventy have to do with vision? Ministry starts and ends with vision. It's probably the most important ingredient in being a redemptive person.

Let's see how it worked. What would have happened if the Lord had given the troops a pop quiz before he lectured about the overripe barley fields?

"All right, men. We're about to ship out. Take out a piece of paper and a pencil and write down the number of folks you think you'll capture for me. Remember, I'm talking about you, not the superstars."

What numbers do you think they would write down? Now shift gears to the present: What would happen if you took the quiz? How many people could God reach through you and your web of relationships? Write down a number.

Apart from a divinely-delivered vision from God, we could total up the projections of the seventy, add yours and mine, and still have counting room on our fingers.

The Lord had to kick out the parameters of their vision, or nothing would have happened. Before they were launched on mission, they needed to see the mission through God's eyes, and base their expectations on God-sized goals.

Successful Evangelism Is the Fruit of Obedience

Don't miss the implications of what might seem an "incidental" comment. The moment the Lord goes on record about the reality of a bountiful harvest, the only options left are belief or unbelief. We either believe him or we don't.

Did Jesus mean that everyone the seventy ran into would be ready to jump on his bandwagon? Hardly. He told them to do a little dust dance in the streets of every town that refused to roll out the red carpet. "Shake a little dust off your feet," he coached them. Rejection? Sure. It goes with the territory. Undoubtedly, some dust got shaken.

But don't forget—*they returned with joy!*

Often we don't obey because we lack faith. There are a couple places our faith gets thin. First, we fear the Lord might not only be right about a ready harvest, he might be asking us to harvest it. Second, we fear that if we try, we'll fail. Somehow we've been robbed of the vision of an enabling God.

Undoubtedly, the ancient leaven of the Sadducees has seeped down through the centuries and polluted the faith of many. The Lord warned the founders of the church about it—it's a vision killer. Sadducees sold their poison in bottles marked "rationalism." They didn't believe in miracles. To them the Resurrection was a historical joke. Ditto all the Lord's miracles. Wasn't life limited to the laws of nature? "God may be real," they said, "but he's not interested in me."

Make no mistake about it, bottled rationalism takes the fizz out of God-sized dreams: "Can't do it, can't afford it, simple as that. Won't work, never has, never will. We tried it once. Besides, it's not in the budget. The sailing's smooth, don't rock the boat. Don't need no faith, we got cash."

When your spiritual bang is limited to bucks, when tapping the supernatural is taboo, the Sadducees have been resurrected (the joke's on them). But without faith, the best we can do is to fire squirt guns at a blazing world. What we see, it seems, is just about what we get.

Successful Evangelism Is the Fruit of Giftedness

Faith and vision are really two sides to the same coin. So what is vision? Vision is a journey into the future. It is a hard climb up a difficult mountain to gain the perspective and wisdom necessary to direct resources and energy to accomplish a worthwhile purpose. Vision looks upward to an almighty God, inward to the divine gifts he has bestowed, and outward to a lost world.

Vision sees God using loaves and fish, if that's what's in my sack. If my sack's got a hammer in it, it sees every nail pounded for the cause of Christ as a tool capable of drawing people toward the Cross. If it's wax in the sack, then vision waxes a neighbor's car.

The faith component of vision says that God will empower my gifts to accomplish his kingdom purposes. Vision involves faith— faith in the unique and special gifting of God, and faith in the enablement and multiplication of those gifts by God.

Let's put the proverbial cards on the table. The Lord is right about the harvest—it is plentiful—and he is asking you to head for the field. Would it alleviate some of your concern to know it's likely that your fear of failure grows out of a common distortion of God's communication strategy?

Without bothering to note the contents of your particular sack, the distorters babble on about how to multiply and serve a cargo of bread and fish. "We'll reach the world," they conclude, "when everyone gets serious about passing out fish and chips."

What they don't see is that chances are good your sack's full of something else. Your instructor's assumption about you is wrong. Those gifted with bread and fish should become the best bread and fish pushers in town. But they shouldn't put a guilt trip on you because your hand fits a wrench.

The missing link in becoming a fully actualized, redemptive person may be a proper vision of God's communication strategy. If we're the lights, what do people see when they see the light? Let's go to Main Street, USA, for our answer.

Effective Evangelism Depends On a Biblical Communication Strategy

It was a fine turnout. Almost 100 percent of the church's membership had shown up to don the signs and stand around the neighborhood. They looked good. Clothes were neat and clean, shoes didn't look too bad, and a few were even smiling. Things were going well.

Hundreds of commuters spotted them standing shoulder to shoulder along the curb facing the traffic. A living picket fence composed of dozens of folks is hard to ignore. This curbside exercise was not so much a protest as a proclamation, for the signs each church member wore shouted, "I am the light of the world."

Those who motored past saw the signs and the saints holding them, but did they see the light? No. Not so much as a glimmer. They saw arms, legs, faces, and signs. They saw the word "light," but they didn't see the Light.

Give the church credit, though. At least the holy huddle had moved outside.

Now reverse the actors in this hypothetical illustration. Plant pagans on the curb, put saints in the cars. What would the saints see? Several dozen folks, some thin, some well dressed, some not so well dressed. Maybe some smiles. They'd see the signs, they'd read the message. But they wouldn't see the light. Even a sober and shaved drunk can carry his "light of the world" sign with some dignity.

What's wrong with this method? Simple. Signs won't convince people they need the Lord. *God's communication strategy has always been to wrap an idea in a person.*

Christ's *life*, John reminds us, was the light. His conduct perfectly revealed his Father's character. Add up his love, holiness, faithfulness, justice, mercy, grace, truth, compassion, etc., and you've described light. "Let your light so shine," our Lord taught, "that they may see your good deeds and praise God in heaven." Note that the Lord invites the world to look, not listen.

Holiness becomes visible through an act of holiness. Faithfulness is hidden until it is made visible through an act of faithfulness. You don't know if I'm compassionate or not until you see me in action.

Christ the Light Modeled a Hands-on Strategy

For thirty-three years, Jesus let the world look as "he made visible the invisible God." Having modeled a communication strategy for us, he passed the torch. "You are the light of the world," he said.

Light is fundamentally a certain kind of life. That's why the commuters saw no light when Christians stood motionless on the curb. When the Lord told his disciples to "let their lights shine," it's likely his mind went back to Isaiah 58.

In that chapter, the prophet explains why God no longer answered the prayers of Israel. He says God's first bride had prostituted herself, had ceased to be the light, and had therefore been rejected. Israel was so blind she could not understand what had happened. She vainly tried to get God's attention. She fasted, and God ignored her. She ripped her garments and threw a fit, and the heavens remained brass. "Why have we fasted," she cried out, "and you have not seen it? Why have we humbled ourselves, and you have not noticed?" (Isaiah 58:3). Somehow, these spiritual exercises didn't impress almighty God.

"You cannot fast as you do today," God reminded them, "and expect your voice to be heard on high" (Isaiah 58:4). So how could they regain God's favor? What set of behaviors would attract the glory of God? When does his light shine? Listen to Isaiah:

> *Is not this the kind of fasting I have chosen: to loose the chains of injustice and untie the cords of the yoke, to set the oppressed free and break every yoke?*
>
> *Is it not to share your food with the hungry and to provide the poor wanderer with shelter—when you see the naked, to clothe him, and not to turn away from your own flesh and blood?*
>
> *Then your light will break forth like the dawn . . . then your righteousness will go before you, and the glory of the LORD will be your rear guard* (Isaiah 58:6-8).

Look at the verbs:

loose	share
untie	provide
set free	clothe
break	not turn away from

Look at the nouns:

chains
yoke

food
shelter
clothing

Light eliminates, liberates, and supplies. When the light's on, the soup's ready and the door is open wide. Look inside the lighthouse! There the hungry are being fed, the naked are being clothed, the imprisoned are being cared for, the discouraged meet a friend, the lonely find a listening ear.

It's then that light explodes in every direction. It breaks forth like the rising sun. Righteousness runs ahead of the true bearer of light, and the unsurpassable glory of God brings up the rear. Isaiah creates a verbal traffic jam describing light. He goes on to say that:

> . . . *if you spend yourselves in behalf of the hungry and satisfy the needs of the oppressed, then your light will rise in the darkness . . .*" (Isaiah 58:10).

Light shines when we use our gifts to meet needs in the name of Christ. Is it any wonder Paul wrote, "I make myself a slave to everyone, to win as many as possible"? (1 Corinthians 9:19). No serving, no winning. Servers win!

"Whoa, brother Aldrich, whoa!" someone says. "All this talk of serving and helping the oppressed sounds a lot like liberalism to me! If you spend your resources doing that sort of thing, in no time at all you forget the gospel! You don't want that, do you?"

No, indeed! We must never forget that it is the gospel, and only the gospel, that saves men and women from hell. We can never forget that. But let me ask you a question: Would you say the apostle Paul was a good role model for evangelism or a bad one?

"That's easy. He was a good one—outside of the Lord, maybe the best!"

Good. I agree. So would you say that following his example leads us to effective evangelism or away from it?

"To it, of course."

I agree again. So if that's true, how do you think we should regard Paul's evangelistic methods as he himself described them?

"I imagine we should imitate them, if we can. But how *does* he describe them?"

I thought you'd never ask. Here's what he wrote in Galatians 2:7-10, a passage describing his unique ministry:

> . . . *they saw that I had been entrusted with the task of preaching the gospel to the Gentiles, just as Peter had been to the Jews. For God, who was at work in the ministry of Peter as an apostle to the Jews, was also at work in my ministry as an apostle to the Gentiles. James, Peter and John, those reputed to be pillars, gave me and Barnabas the right hand of fellowship when they recognized the grace given to me. They agreed that we should go to the Gentiles, and they to the Jews. All they asked was that we should continue to remember the poor, the very thing I was eager to do.*

Did you catch that last line? How did Paul, a premier example of effective evangelism, regard serving the needs of the poor? Did he say he left it to others? Did he say he concentrated on preaching, lest by serving the poor he should forget the gospel?

No. He said he would "continue to remember the poor." And how would he do that? By meeting their needs. By serving them. By involving himself in their physical well-being. To get a picture of how this concern worked itself out in practical terms, read 2 Corinthians 8-9.

Notice, too, that this phase of Paul's ministry was something he described as "the *very thing* I am *eager* to do." He not only did it—he singled it out as one activity he loved doing.

One last observation: Note that it wasn't just Paul who thought it wise to pursue this kind of ministry. The mandate came from the very "pillars of the church": It was Peter and James and John whom Paul said "*asked* that we should continue to remember the poor." Were all four of these men confused, or were they on to something?

I'll bet you know what I think.

A Modern-day Example

It was time for the second session to begin, and before the moderator turned the session over to me, he asked if he could give his testimony. I nodded.

"While listening to Joe speak on effective evangelism," he said, "I was reminded of my pilgrimage to the foot of the Cross. I was driving through town on a Sunday morning, and wouldn't you know it, my car broke down . . . right in front of a church. Wasn't much I could do. I popped my hood open and waited. I didn't know much about the Bible, but I did remember the parable of the good Philippian. Surely, someone from the church would help.

"Eventually, church was over and the doors opened. Folks streamed past the pastor at the Glorifying Of The Worm ceremony and flooded down the steps past me. Nobody stopped. Nobody asked any questions or offered to help. I was getting madder by the minute.

"Finally, the last saint disappeared, the pastor locked

the door, came down the steps toward the car, and inno-
cently asked 'What seems to be the problem?' I shared
with him a piece of my mind I could ill afford to lose.

"'But sir,' he protested, 'I'd like to help. I have mechan-
ical abilities. I can fix your car, but not today; you'll have
to wait until tomorrow.'

"I thought he was mocking me. What does a pastor
know about automobiles? 'Oh sure,' I said. 'Why don't
you come on over for breakfast, too, while you're at it?'

"'Great,' he said, 'What time do you want me to show
up?'

"'Make it 8:00,' I said, no way expecting him to show.
He did. I was still in bed. He tackled the car like he
knew what he was doing. He knew how to use the tools.
Even got grease under his fingernails. This was no wimp!

"This reverend spent most of the day under the hood
of my car. I wondered why a total stranger would give
his day off to fix my car, solving my problem. I figured
anybody who'd care enough to fix a stranger's car just
might have something to say. He wouldn't let me pay
him, so I figured I should at least show up for church. I
did. He preached, I came forward, and was saved. Now
I'm a 'reverend,' all because someone used his talents to
meet my needs . . . a broken car and a broken heart."

This man saw the Light because someone fixed a trans-
mission. It was a wrench in the preacher's sack that
prepared a sinner to meet the Bread of Life.

Biblical Metaphors Shape
Successful Evangelism Strategy

God's communication strategy, modeled by Christ and
illustrated by the mechanic-pastor, is supported by several
significant metaphors. Let's check out some of these word

pictures and continue to sharpen our vision of how God communicates through us.

1. A *living epistle, read by all men* (2 Corinthians 3:2, 3).

Paul tells us evangelism is allowing the non-Christian to turn the pages of your life and read the fine print. This imagery presupposes regular, close contact with non-Christians. As a general rule, however, Christians gild the cover and conceal the contents.

Open or closed, the response to the Christ of the Bible is often determined by the material found in the book of our lives.

2. A *shining star* (Philippians 2:15)

Paul's use of this picture reminds us that our appeal is not simply intellectual or theological. Our goal is not to beat people into submission by whipping their arguments. A star- studded sky, like a community salted with Christians, appeals to the aesthetic part of man. Beauty has always been central to God's evangelism enterprise. A starlit night leaves us breathless. Something deep inside is stirred as we compare ourselves to the vastness of space.

"When I consider your heavens, the work of your fingers, the moon and the stars, which you have set in place, what is man that you are mindful of him?" asks David in Psalm 8:3-4. The heavens, we are told, declare the glory of God. So do his living stars.

3. A *fragrant aroma* (2 Corinthians 2:15).

Perfume short-circuits the intellect and captures the heart. Influence nonbelievers like perfume influences you! Again, we're talking about something aesthetically pleasing. The redemptive neighbor is winsome. He has a distinctive, attractive fragrance which stands out from the aromas of this world. He's the aroma of life to those who believe, and the aroma of death to those who reject Christ. The only essence that captures attention comes from the Father. We're to be God-scented people!

4. A *wise fisherman* (Matthew 4:19).

"Fishers of men," we're called by our Master. Not hunters. Hunters ambush Bambi on the way to the water hole. Fishermen select an appropriate lure for a specific species. They know their habitat as well as their habits. They know fish.

With Nicodemus, the master Fisherman talked of a new birth, a highly metaphorical term appropriate for theologians. Beside a well on a hot day, he spoke of thirst. Observing the Feast of Lights, he contrasted light and darkness and proclaimed himself the Light of the world.

5. A *beautiful bride* (Ephesians 5:25-33).

This potent imagery highlights the testimony of a particular local church or group of believers. Beauty attracts people to the truth. Is there any better symbol of beauty than a bride adorned for her beloved? Brides turn macho men of steel into jelly. Hearts are moved, emotions stirred when a bride walks down the aisle. We're talking about curb appeal!

The bride was beautiful in Acts 2. Her sacrificial generosity turned people's heads, believers and unbelievers alike. And, please note, "the Lord added to their number daily those who were being saved" (Acts 2:47). Churches must qualify for the blessing of God. He doesn't put healthy babies in disease-ridden incubators.

6. *Salt* (Matthew 5:13).

What's one four-letter word unfortunately missing from the experience of many believers? S-A-L-T. Both Paul and the Lord use the imagery of salt to underscore the necessity of believers remaining flavorful while maintaining contact with unbelievers. They warn us that although there is no impact without contact, contact may lead to compromise or loss of flavor. Our mission is to bring holiness (flavor) to embittered palates.

7. Light (Matthew 5:14).

Light speaks of God's character revealed through the believer's life. One purpose of this light is to expose the realities of darkness. The problem of unused light is not compromise, but concealment; not loss of flavor, but loss of visibility. It was inconceivable to our Lord that we would put our light under a bushel. How do we do that? Among other things, we do it when we compromise our testimony or when we shut ourselves off from non-Christians.

8. A *patient farmer* (Matthew 13:1-43).

Agricultural imagery is the major metaphor Christ used to help us grasp his communication strategy. We're to be like farmers who cultivate, sow, and reap. The first two parables of Matthew 13 teach us that every soul without Christ is a soil to be cultivated, and every soul with Christ is a seed to be planted.

Good seed, mind you. The word for good is the Greeks' favorite term for beauty. God is sowing beautiful people in his world. The effective evangelist must take seriously the quality of the soil and the quality of the seed. Christians with an ugly, ungodly disposition do not help the cause of Christ. The farmer tends a soul, hovering over it, pulling weeds, breaking up hard soil, chasing away robber birds.

Our Lord uses the harvest imagery in a startling comment to his disciples as recorded in John 4. He'd just scandalized them by evangelizing the Samaritan woman bound for the well, and then he tells them, "I'm sending you out to reap what you have not sown. *Others have done the hard labor.*"

Read that again. Do you understand what he said?

Reaping isn't all there is to evangelism. In fact, reaping isn't even the hard labor. Any farmer knows that. It takes one day to harvest what you've cultivated and nurtured for months. Furthermore, the disciples were going to reap a harvest they hadn't sown. "I planted," Paul said, "Apollos watered, and God gave the increase." Paul handed off some souls to Apollos. God gave the increase. The soil must be cultivated, the seed planted and nurtured, and then comes the harvest.

Another Modern-day Example

A llama farmer in Sisters, Oregon, loved a scruffy little town character for more than sixteen years. A pastor friend of mine recently moved into the community, met this town mascot, and led him to Christ. My friend reaped a well-cultivated soul. A group of us had lunch some time later, and my friend asked an interesting question.

"Who," he asked, "do you think led that man to the Lord, the llama farmer or me?" Rising to the occasion, one of our group responded, "the llama farmer." "No," replied the pastor, "neither of us did. Whenever a person is saved, it is always the Body of Christ that leads him to the foot of the Cross."

I like that! In most conversion stories, there's a grandmother who prayed, a parent who lived right, a peer who spoke, a pastor who proclaimed, an author who wrote, an evangelist who appealed, a friend who listened, and others who served. The souls I've been privileged to "harvest" were the result of the hard labor of many faithful believers.

Adult minds aren't like those of children. Children's minds are like screen doors, easily opened and easily closed. They're believers by nature. Adult minds are more like bank vault doors. It takes patience, time, and lots of love to get those doors swinging on their hinges.

So what does this mean to you? God may have called you to be a cultivator, to do the hard labor. Your sack possibly contains a pick and shovel, not a tract or a gospel presentation. *Do what God has gifted you to do.* Refuse to feel guilty because you're not a reaper. Remember, that's the easy part. Try loosing, untying, setting free, breaking, sharing, providing, and clothing. Do it deliberately, with evangelism in mind. Then stand back, because your light will shine, shine, shine. Serve to win!

Successful Evangelism Is a Three-phase Process

God's communication strategy is to wrap ideas in people and turn them loose to cultivate, sow, and reap. The cultivation and sowing end of the process majors in making truth visible; the reaping end leans toward making truth audible. The one demonstrates, the other explains. Both are important. Let's take a look at these three phases, one at a time.

1. Cultivation is an appeal to the heart through the building of a relationship.

Cultivation isn't a relationship with a hook. Quite frankly, I don't want to be your project. You probably don't want to be mine, either. It's worth your time to build a relationship with nonbelievers even if they never trust the Lord. Why? Because they are made in the image and likeness of God. They're not pets or trees or flowers.

A friendship reduces relationship tension, eliminates caricatures, builds trust, and opens hearts to consider Christ. The pre-Christian wants to know what kind of people he'll be joining if he becomes a Christian. She wants to know what kind of an outfit she's getting into before she makes any commitments. That's one reason most phone campaigns aren't effective. While thousands have professed to receive Christ over the phone, virtually none ever show up in church. Why not? They don't know what to expect. A good Christian friend is a sample to the pre-Christian of what's to come.

The effectiveness of cultivation depends upon the personality and reputation of the cultivator. It would be best for a surly, self-righteous Christian never to open his mouth or "share Christ."

Research indicates that effective communication is 7 percent verbal, 38 percent tone of voice, and 55 percent nonverbal. We often say, "It's not what you said that upset me, it's how you said it." There was nothing irritating about the words; it was the impudent tone of voice, the defiant posture, the look of disdain which fired our tempers. Any hint of a judgmental or superior attitude immediately jeopardizes the verbal message, however true that message may be.

The ancient Greeks said effective communicators had three qualities: ethos, pathos, and logia. Ethos speaks of *character*. It is the root word for our term "ethics." Believers must be ethical, men and women of character. But that's not enough. People of integrity who lack *compassion* (pathos) can be as cold as ice. God's frozen people, we call them. Pathos is the root of our words "empathy" and "sympathy." People really don't care how much you know until they know how much you care. There is a direct correlation between the assurance of love and the acceptance of truth.

Logia, a term which we translate "word," reminds us that character and compassion are not enough. Effective communication must have *content.* It must be verbalized. Evangelism is both "show" and "tell." Those gifted in reaping have the ability to verbalize the content of the gospel, while cultivators demonstrate it. Cultivators put on the soup, reapers pull out the Scriptures. Cultivators appeal to the heart, reapers appeal to the will. Cultivators display, reapers proclaim.

2. *Sowing is an appeal to the mind through the communication of revelation.*

In the sowing phase of evangelism, the goal is to expose the pre-Christian to the fundamental concepts of the Christian faith. People should make informed decisions. An intelligent decision is based upon accurate information. Research indicates that those who trust the Lord and remain as members of the church have had over five exposures to the gospel before they received Christ. Those who "trust Christ" and drop out had no more than two exposures to the gospel.

Sowers are seed planters, sensitive to the readiness of the soil. In the realm of spiritual nurture, cultivation and sowing often happen at the same time. We break up packed earth and plant seeds simultaneously.

Seeds take many forms: A word of testimony, a simple comment, a tract or book, an evangelistic event, a radio or TV program, a note or letter. The things offered may relate to a felt need and have little to do with the gospel *per se.*

When you deal in basic needs, you're always valued. It may be that a book on marriage and family may start someone on the path toward trusting Christ. Perhaps a James Dobson film series or a cassette tape will be used by God to bring them to Christ. In order for that to happen, however, a Christian must be there, know what the need is, and meet it.

3. *Reaping is an appeal to the will in anticipation of a response.*

The pre-Christian has heard the music of the gospel played by the cultivators and sowers. Now he is ready for the words. He's asking the reason for the hope he has observed. Reaping is responding to the Philippian jailer when he cried out "Sirs, what must I do to be saved?"

Is evangelism warming up the soup? No, but that's part of it.

Is evangelism passing out a tract? No, but that's part of it.

Is evangelism what Billy Graham does? That's part of it.

Evangelism is a process through which people flow toward the foot of the Cross. Along the way, there are many influences which God brings to bear. All work to bring that person to the point where "God gives the increase." Sometimes we reap what others have sown, other times we sow what others reap. We'll develop these three phases of evangelism—cultivating, sowing, reaping—later on.

Wrapping Up

Freddy the frog was stuck in an impossible rut. He couldn't get out. His friends offered all kinds of advice, but to no avail. He was stuck. His friends left him alone and went about their business.

Some time later they remembered Freddy's dilemma

and returned to check on him. Peering over the edge, their eyes rolled from one end of the rut to the other and saw nothing. Freddy wasn't in the rut. This made them both excited and concerned—excited that he'd gotten out, but concerned about what might have happened. They sent out search parties to find their missing friend.

Finally he was located. A signal flare shot up, and frogs came from everywhere to be reunited with their friend. It was a joyful, chaotic reunion. Everyone was croaking and hopping at once. Finally a leader frog held up his flipper and quieted the crowd.

"Freddy," he said, "it's so good to see you! We thought you were caught in an impossible rut. How'd you get out?"

"Well, fellow frogs," Freddy replied, "I *was* caught in an impossible rut, but a big Mack truck came along and I had to get out."

A rut is a grave with both ends kicked out. If you're rooting around in a rut, maybe God's got a big Mack truck coming your way. Let's hope so!

The fields are white, and you've been drafted. Look in your sack. You can feed yourself, or bless five, fifty, or five thousand others.

Ministry begins with an inventory of your talents. Your talents are the clue to where you fit in the process of evangelism. Your faith in your co-laborer, God, is what enables you to escape the sorry Sadducees and to dream God-sized dreams.

So where do you go from here?

Read on!

Know your enemy and his tactics.

3

SCOUTING THE OTHER TEAM

How do you exasperate the Little Red Hen? By slipping some duck eggs in her nest. I know, I've done it. She'll keep those eggs toasty warm until those little peepers and quackers hatch. And then the fun begins.

A puddle or pond is all it takes to separate the chickens from the ducks. Eyes round with terror, the Little Red Hen watches the aquatic part of her brood frolic recklessly in and under the water. Her mind can't compute what her eyes are telling her. Chickens don't swim!

In a feathered frenzy, she paces the shore, hoping to avert a disaster. She scolds and pleads to no avail. Her water-soaked charges not only guzzle the liquid, they bathe, swim, and play submarine in the stuff. Nothing seems to dampen their enthusiasm.

Mom's counsel has a shelf-life about the length of a sparkling droplet on a busy duck's back. Shore-bound by nature, her chicken brain cannot resolve the mystery of her water-bound step-children. She's been deceived.

There's some good advice in this parable for anyone involved in evangelism. Before you find a nest and sit on it, it's best to know what's in there. To be forewarned is to be forearmed. Not everyone is going to be excited about your evangelistic agenda. Jesus told the seventy:

> *The harvest is plentiful, but the workers are few. Ask the Lord of the harvest, therefore, to send out workers into his harvest field. Go! I am sending you out like lambs among wolves* (Luke 10:2-3).

Down through the centuries, the Lord's voice continues to say, "Go, I am sending you, and you, and you," . . . and the wolves bare their fangs. Every venture must wrestle with the tension between *opportunity* (a plentiful harvest) and *opposition* (the wolves). The objective is to harvest the harvest. To do that successfully, the opposition (the wolf pack) must be overcome.

The Disloyal Opposition

"Your objective, gentlemen, is to harvest a crop," Jesus says. "The opposition is determined to abort your mission." In Jesus' imagery, the wolf pack stands between the sheep and the harvest field, between the believer and his non-Christian friends.

Notice carefully that wolves attack in two directions: the ripening fields and those who come to harvest—the harvester and the harvestee, if you will. Part of the problem we have in harvesting grows out of Satan's blinding of the lost. The lost are blind. Furthermore, they've been trapped and taken captive.

Our goal is to help them "come to their senses and *escape from the trap of the devil*, who has taken· them captive to do his will" (2 Timothy 2:26). The wolf pack's objective is to stop the harvest from taking place. They've been remarkably successful. So who are these wolves? What do they look like? And how do they operate?

Who Are the Wolves?

There are at least three ways to identify the wolves. First, the wolves could refer to *unbelievers* in general. In that case, the Lord is telling the seventy that they are being sent out into communities where all unbelievers are to be viewed as wolves. "It's us against the wolves," would be the idea.

The Lord, however, refers to the five thousand bread-fed folks as "sheep without a shepherd" in Mark 6:34. Even though most of them were unsaved, he called them "lost sheep," not wolves. Furthermore, when the Lord sent out the twelve, he told them to go "to the lost sheep of Israel" (Matthew 10:6). In most cases, the non-Christian is not the enemy, he's the victim of the enemy.

Second, wolves may be *false teachers*. The Lord warned his disciples to "watch out for false prophets. They come to you in sheep's clothing, but inwardly they are ferocious wolves" (Matthew 7:15).

Third, the wolves can symbolize the *forces of the evil one*. We know that before the Lord sent out the seventy, he warned them about "wolves." When they returned, they reported, "Lord, even the demons submit to us in your name" (Luke 10:17). They got the point: wolves = demons.

The immediate context supports the idea that the Lord's warning about wolves is primarily a reference to the forces of hell. The king of the pack, Satan, transforms himself into an angel of light and comes in the guise of goodness and right. It's a tremendous strategy—an angel of light appeals to us, it fits well within the general framework of Christian thinking. Deception is the most powerful weapon in the satanic arsenal.

No ugly, sinister monster is going to materialize and attempt to dissuade you from reaching your neighbors. Angels don't growl, snap, and chew. No, at times the deceiver will take the "nice guy, don't rock the boat approach." He'll patronize us into complacency by suggesting some good Christian excuses:

Nobody else is doing it; why should you? [generally a true statement].

Your family is first [basically true].

It's god [he wouldn't use a capital letter] who gives the increase, not me [not bad!].

I'm too busy [probably true].

I'm not able to talk to strangers about spiritual things [one of his favorites].

God is more interested in "being" than "doing" [it's got a ring of truth to it . . . not bad].

I've got to go "deep" for a while [probably not true].

Let Billy Graham do it [makes sense, doesn't it?].

My own life is too screwed up [and it may well be].

God's going to save everyone, anyway, so why get worked up about it [definitely not true].

Or:

Luke 9:59: "Lord, first let me go and bury my father" [sounds reasonable].

Luke 9:61: "I will follow you Lord; but first let me go back and say good-by to my family" [good stuff].

Jonah: "I don't like the Assyrians" [or name the group].

If sweet-talking doesn't work, the tyrant hurls flaming arrows. He jumps right into the middle of the sheepfold, sword swinging, and literally raises hell. He comes, according to our Shepherd, "to steal and kill and destroy" (John 10:10). He comes to steal from us all that is good and right and true. Now ugly as sin, he comes to take life away, to move us toward death in our marriages, families, and relationships. He comes to destroy all that God has built, to tear down the work God has begun. If he can't talk us out of reaching out to the lost, he will try to destroy all that is right and good about us and compromise the name of Christ through us.

If neither of these work, if he can't patronize or tyrannize us, he'll attempt to neutralize us by focusing on our failures. The mud-slinger knows the way to the garbage dump. Furthermore, he knows how to resurrect the stuff . . . *our* stuff. He gets to us in spite of the fact that we know our dump is posted "No Trespassing." Can you hear him?

What makes you think God can use someone like you to evangelize folks? You're no better than they are. Look at the garbage. God doesn't use junk. At least wait until you get your act together. The world hates hypocrites, you know.

Confused because there is truth in what he whispers, we hesitate. Like a guided missile, he zeroes in on our convictions about God and his goodness. He questions the motives of God. He suggests that God's plan is restrictive and narrow.

Having "girded our loins with truth," we stand and fight, taking the great doctrines of God and his love out of mothballs and hurling them back at him. But his relentless accusations confuse us, our convictions falter, and he enters phase two of his attack. He attempts to destroy our confidence by throwing our shame at us. The garbage *is* ours. No doubt about it. And it's rotten.

Convictions, confidence, courage. If we lose the first two, we've lost the third. That's what Satan wants.

Have you ever felt unworthy to witness? We all have. So how do we withstand Satan's reminder of our unrighteousness? Our answer is a piece of armor mentioned in Ephesians 6: The breastplate of righteousness, *Christ's* righteousness. Satan talks about righteousness, too—about our lack of it. He just neglects to mention the imputation of Christ's righteousness to our account.

Another line of defense is to have on the right war boots. Our feet must be shod with the preparation that a full understanding of the gospel of peace provides.

How's the Enemy Doing?

Can we take stock of our enemy's success? How has the imitation angel done? Do you know many Christians who are actively reaching their neighbors and friends for Christ? Is Satan keeping you from being a redemptive neighbor through any of his tricks?

The devil's game plan is to get you out of the game any way he can. To do that, he's recruited some help. He isn't the only quick change artist you'll come up against.

Our Lord said that heretics come to us in sheep's clothing. Lambskin clerics, if you please. They, too, have retractable fangs. A sheep is a sheep when it eats grass, grows wool, and bleats a lot. But a sheep is not always a sheep in the sanctuary (or in the seminary, for that matter).

Lanolin smooth, they sit in the pew or wag their tails on the platform every Sunday. Often these mongrels are two-faced. They pass the plate and invest the proceeds. Others preach pious platitudes which amount to deep fog in the area of the crucial. Most of them are nice guys.

Paul referred to such heretics as wolves: "I know that after I leave, savage wolves will come in among you and will not spare the flock. Even from your own number men will arise and distort the truth in order to draw away disciples after them" (Acts 20:29-30).

Just this week I saw an advertisement for a new book which called for "a bold new vision for the church: a vision that affirms gay rights, divorce, and sexual activity outside of marriage between committed, responsible adults." The book, called an example of "courageous thinking" by its publisher, was written by a bishop of a large denomination. The ad called him "a controversial churchman." Paul might have called him a wolf.

Wolves not only lead the flock astray, they prevent Christians from becoming redemptive people. By propagating falsehood, by pushing ideas that stand opposed to a biblical way of life, they sideline Christians who should be in the battle. They say things like:

> Christ is nice, sin is unfortunate, and to preach only one way of salvation is too narrow. Sincerity is the supreme virtue. Love is inclusive; let's forget "holiness." The Bible? Pre-scientific. A commendable, fallible record of the religious experience of others. The gospel? To be "saved" [not one of their favorite terms] is to be liberated from oppressive political structures. The blood? Please, don't talk about the blood. It's a remnant from primitive religion.

Fact of the matter is, friends, some of you attend churches where the gospel is not preached, where ministers are traitors to the cause of Christ. You will pay a price in those churches if you take the problem of the lost seriously and get on board to be part of the solution. The struggle is real, the enemy is powerful, the price is high.

For God's sake, pay the price!

What about the Sheep?

I'm tired of talking about wolves. The Lord likened his friends to baby sheep. We can learn from this analogy. Maybe our old friends Amos and Zechariah can help.

"Amos, I don't like this stuff he's saying about wolves and lambs."

"I know just what you mean. The odds aren't too encouraging. I'm all for ministry, you know, but couldn't he fix the fight, or even up the odds a bit? Besides, I'm no lamb."

"Exactly! I'd feel a lot better if he'd say he's sending us out as coyotes among the wolves."

"Maybe then we'd have a chance!"

"Right. At least a coyote's got teeth. He can chew on a hind leg or something before he's done in."

"Yea, but lambs? When the wolf pack hits, there'll be fur and lamb chops flying in every direction."

"It's a shame, a dirty shame."

Hold on, folks! Maybe being a lamb isn't as bad as it looks. Can we learn something from the lamb label, besides that we're vulnerable? Perhaps Napoleon, an old hand at warfare, can help.

Napoleon claimed that *a man becomes the man of his uniform.* Christ sent the seventy out and identified them as lambs, and there are some interesting questions about his choice of terms. Is he sending us out as lambs because that is what we are, or is he sending us out under the mandate to become lambs so that we would serve others with the attitude and qualities of a lamb?

Is the key to victory vulnerability? Is the Lord saying, "you're lambs going against wolves," or "you are to become lambs to overcome the wolves"? The text's grammar will support either option.

It's an interesting paradox. We are vulnerable, and to be strong, we must be vulnerable. We are weak when we are strong, and strong when we are weak.

It is my opinion that being a lamb is both a *description* and a *destination.* Yes, we are sheep. We are also to become like sheep.

Is the Lord suggesting that all of the "wolfishness" is not yet removed from his sheep? Is he suggesting that his lambs may want to fight fire with fire? "Snap at me, friend, and I'll bare my fangs!"

Although we are new creatures in Christ, it's human nature to revert to past identities when we're under stress. Accused by a woman, Peter swore like a fisherman. "If you," Paul wrote, "keep on biting and devouring each other, watch out or you will be destroyed by each other" (Galatians 5:15).

I don't think sheep bite.

So, what are sheep like? What is the identity you must assume to be a strong, redemptive person? Let's look at some redemptive qualities which characterize those whom God uses.

Persuasive Sheep Are Defenseless

To survive, sheep must be defended by something other than fellow sheep. Because of their vulnerability, sheep must trust and obey. They have no option. Because they are defenseless, they are dependent creatures. They can't make it without the wisdom and strength of the shepherd. They're cute little rascals, but good looks won't pass muster when the pack appears. They can be charmers, but a persuasive personality isn't enough.

Persuasive Sheep Are Gentle

Sheep aren't rough, assertive, overbearing. That's why to truly become a lamb is a miracle. We're basically self-centered and pushy. Listen to Paul describe those who qualify for Christian leadership:

> *Now the overseer must be above reproach . . . self-controlled, respectable, hospitable, . . . not violent but gentle, not quarrelsome, not a lover of money. He must also have a good reputation with outsiders, so that he will not fall into disgrace and into the devil's trap* (1 Timothy 3:2-3,7).

Notice some other references to this quality of gentleness:

> *Be completely humble and gentle; be patient, bearing with one another in love* (Ephesians 4:2).

> *. . . but we were gentle among you*
> *(1 Thessalonians 2:7).*

> *. . . gentleness [a fruit of the Spirit]* (Galatians 5:23).

> *And the Lord's servant must not quarrel; instead he must be kind to everyone, able to teach, not resentful. Those who oppose him he must gently instruct, in the*

hope that God will grant them [a change of heart] leading them to a knowledge of the truth, and that they will come to their senses and escape from the trap of the devil, who has taken them captive to do his will (2 Timothy 2:24-26).

. . . show true humility toward all men (Titus 3:2).

. . . learn from me, for I am gentle and humble in heart (Matthew 11:29).

Blessed are the meek . . . (Matthew 5:5).

Your goal isn't to enter into a battle with non-Christians and "win." Not if "winning" means to beat them down with rhetoric or logic. Yes, we should be logical. Gentle instruction is not devoid of content.

That content is enhanced, however, if it is communicated with gentleness and grace. "Speaking the truth in love" is the key. Love without truth is mushy sentimentality. Truth without love is brutality. The flavor of our life is to be gentle, and when we communicate verbally, our vocal intonation, our tone of voice, our body language, all are to reflect that gentleness of spirit. Billy Graham communicates powerfully but has a gentle spirit.

Gentleness under pressure, and meekness in the midst of pain caused a hardened Roman centurion to declare, "truly, this was the Son of God."

Peter reminds us that it was Christ's giving up his right to retaliate that caused many to return "to the Shepherd and Overseer" of their souls. "When they hurled their insults at him," Peter explains, "he did not retaliate; when he suffered, he made no threats" (1 Peter 2:23, 25).

Gentleness and composure in the midst of stress and pain is a powerful component of effective communication. When the non-believer sees you responding to adversity with gentleness, he will "ask you to give the reason for the hope that you have" (1 Peter 3:15). He's heard the music of the gospel and wants to hear the words. How do you respond?

Always be prepared to give an answer to everyone who asks you to give the reason for the hope that you have. But do this with gentleness and respect . . ." (1 Peter 3:15).

Unfortunately, when Christians switch from talking about football to talking about Christ, they often kick into a "religious twang" or a "stained-glass voice." It doesn't help. Sometimes they flip their argument switch when the subject touches religion, as though evangelism were an intellectual wrestling match. We argue as though Jesus needed defending. We do it, I think, because our ego is at stake, and we must engage and defeat the adversary at all costs. We wind up shooting ourselves in the foot.

Generally speaking, a highly argumentative nonbeliever isn't anywhere near the Cross. Entering into heated debate with him will drive him further away. Gently tell such a one to go, sell all he has, and give it to the poor. If he sticks around and persists in debate, tell him, "I know how you feel, but isn't it wonderful that God loves you and has a plan for your life?" Watch him melt.

There's a basic principle of communication interwoven in this discussion. The louder the noise, the weaker the argument. That's why a confident, gentle spirit can be so powerful. It exasperates the opposition. Your opponent wants you to join him in the shout and shove match. Don't! You both lose. Wives who have spiritually indifferent husbands are told they can win them without a word (1 Peter 3:1-4). The supernatural wardrobe of a "meek and quiet spirit" can do what nothing else can.

Persuasive Sheep Live Sacrificial Lives

Sheep aren't harnessed to pull wagons or to plow fields. They aren't used for home protection. You don't saddle sheep, either. The fact is, sheep aren't worth much when they're alive. Their whole life they prepare for death, at which time they become wool and leg of lamb. You might say they spend their lives as "living sacrifices."

In the Old Testament sacrificial system, sheep died so others could live. In the New Testament, believers are called "living sacrifices." To be a living sacrifice is to die to self and live for others.

It's to say "no" to some good things to say "yes" to God's agenda.

It's to take off a Monday afternoon and fix a stranger's car.

It's to take over a meal when you feel like eating out.

It's to listen when your mind wants to race in a thousand directions.

It's to spend hours with the players, coaches, and team when you'd rather be fishing.

It's to attend community meetings when you'd rather be home.

It's to be involved in parties and neighborhood events when you'd prefer to read a good novel.

It's to open your home to people whose habits offend you, whose language is ungodly.

It's to invest money, time, and energy into something other than your version of the American Dream.

It's to choose inconvenience over convenience, chaos

over serenity, risk over safety.

It's to choose obedience over disobedience.

Paul put it this way: "I make myself a servant to everyone, *to win as many as possible*" (1 Corinthians 9:19). NO SERVING, NO WINNING.

People hear the music of the gospel and see its light when Christians serve. Ultimately, we are towel wearers and basin bearers. Not doctors. Not lawyers. Not mothers. Not shop workers. Those on God's best-dressed list don't need anything from Neiman Markup. They'll be wearing frayed, worn-out towels.

I can't begin to tell you how critical it is that for your sake and for the sake of your family, community, and world, that you discover you are a servant. Period. All other credentials are just that, credentials. Your identity is not to center around your profession, but around your divine calling.

Are you serving? That's what cultivating is all about. It's appealing to the heart through the building of a relationship.

Now, you can be a servant and get paid for what you do. God isn't expecting us to forgo remuneration. That's not the issue. I know some who perform for nothing and aren't servants. On the other hand, you could charge a fortune for your skills and still perform with the heart and soul of a servant. Servants do things for others, but they do them with a distinctive attitude.

What kind of attitude?

It's an attitude of gentleness which affirms the value and worth of the other. It's an attitude of humility which considers others to be better than one's self. It's service with no strings attached. It's service motivated by love. It's using your skills and abilities to meet the needs of others, with no expectation of reciprocity. It's yielding your agenda to the agenda of others.

It's an attitude whose origin is supernatural.

None of us are servants by nature. We wouldn't have washed feet, either. Lambs make sacrifices. They are called to give their lives away in the service of others. It's a high and holy calling—and an exceptionally difficult one. Check your uniform.

Persuasive Sheep Are Powerful

Sheep are, indeed, the most powerful tools in God's arsenal. God's winning strategy is to hit the battlefield with U.S.D.A. choice lambs, and win. Think about the great leaders of Christendom. Almost without exception, they are people of great humility. Strange, isn't it, that the way up with God is always down? "Humble yourselves, therefore, under God's mighty hand, that he may lift you up in due time" says Peter (1 Peter 5:6).

More than anything else, humility involves the yielding of rights. As we yield rights, God releases power. As we assert our rights, he removes power. Notice how Paul dealt with the issue of rights in 1 Corinthians 9:4-19:

> Don't we have the right to food and drink?
> Don't we have the right to take a believing wife along with us?
> Who serves as a soldier at his own expense?
> If others have this right of support from you, shouldn't we have it all the more?

> But . . .

> we did not use this right (these rights).
> On the contrary, we put up with anything rather than hinder the gospel of Christ.

I make myself a slave to everyone, to win as many as possible.

Servants are powerful precisely because they have abandoned their rights. To be redemptive people in the office, home, or family, we must adjust all priorities to divine specifications. They must reflect his agenda, not ours. It's a tough assignment.

Sure, we all have a right to Monday night football. We have a right to be with our family and friends, to travel, play, and rest. No doubt about it. But something has to give if we are going to impact our generation. More about that later!

What Help Can We Expect?

It may be that after you better understand what a lamb is and does, you're not too excited about becoming one. Nobody really relishes the thought of becoming the featured entree for a pack of snarling wolves.

But before you relegate those vulnerable fur-balls to the supermarket, try this on for size. Visualize a four-footed, wool-covered bag of butterfat waddling up a gravel path toward a huge gate in a solid stone wall. A sign over the gate says "Ephesians 6: God's armament depot."

The gate swings open. Our sheep tiptoes over the threshold as the gate closes behind him. Some time later another gate opens farther down the wall. Trumpets sound, lights flash, bells ring. There's our friend, bigger than life, decked out with a sword, the breastplate of righteousness, and the helmet of salvation. He's got sheepskin seat covers and steel wool.

He's an attack lamb!

Fur slicked back with lanolin, he's ready to move on out. Ever seen a God-armored, sword-swinging lamb pack rout a flock of wolves?

It can happen—but do you know why roaring lions flee and wolves scatter? It's not because they're afraid of lambs. It's the shepherd they can't get along with.

Jesus told us to "pray the *Lord* of the harvest to thrust forth laborers into *his* harvest field." He's the Lord of the harvest in your neighborhood, office, or barbershop, and it's his harvest field. The wolf pack must yield to the Shepherd. When the Shepherd says, "Go, I am sending you," sent ones go under the protective shield of his commission and his enablement.

The Lord's comparison between lambs and wolves was carefully chosen. The odds were hopeless—*they always are when we trust anyone or anything but the Shepherd.*

Jesus has promised us a lot of help, both in person and through some major-league personal representatives. So who's on our team?

Elisha's servant wondered the same thing. One morning he went out to get the *Dothan Daily News* and found the town surrounded by bounty hunters looking for Elisha. It was tremble time . . . but not for the old prophet.

"Oh, my Lord," cried the servant, "what shall we do?"

"Don't be afraid," the prophet replied. "Those who are with us are more than those who are with them."

What did Elisha mean? It was prophet and servant against an army of soldiers, horses, and chariots big enough to surround the city! Any fool could see that! Elisha prayed:

*"O LORD, open his eyes so he may see." Then the Lord opened the servant's eyes, and he looked and saw the hills full of horses and **chariots of fire** all around Elisha* (2 Kings 6:17).

Chariots of fire, surrounding Elisha! Just a whisper away stood the battle-ready cavalry of God Almighty.

My friend, they're still there! Do you see the chariots, smell the fire? It looks like you and I are alone against the wolf pack. It appears that we're outnumbered in our office, tennis club, and neighborhood. The laborers are few and far between. The majority rules . . . or so it seems.

My friend, I can't tell you how important it is for you to visualize the army of God surrounding you and the harvest field to which he has called you. We're laborers together with the *Lord* of the harvest, sent out by him into *his* harvest field.

With these kind of odds, we begin to expect results, and results begin to happen. Elisha knew he needed the chariots. He knew they were there when he needed them. May God give you the same assurance!

So What Do We Do Now?

Let's get back to Amos and Zechariah for a moment. It sounds like they've been discussing their situation.

"Sent like sheep among the wolves. So that's about it, huh?"

"I don't know how else to put it."

"So, how do we track a wolf?"

"I guess we're supposed to read their footprints. Look for complacency—a 'who cares' attitude, or busy-ness."

"Could lack of confidence be a footprint? Wasn't that the trouble with Elisha's servant?"

"I think so. He didn't see the chariots of fire. He

was probably guilty of unbelief. Let's hope he remembered the chariots in time."

"'Remember the chariots.' Not a bad slogan! Aren't wolf tracks often spotted in Christian relationships? Lots of good soldiers get done in on the home front."

"Yeah, they do great on the battlefield but get cratered at home. Compromise is another telltale wolf sign."

"That's good to remember. So what should we do now?"

"Let's go hunting."

Amos and Zechariah sound ready for their adventure. How about you? Could you use a few more pointers? Let me offer several for those who are wondering what to do now.

1. Accept the commission.

Sign on board. Tell the Lord that by his grace you'll identify a network of people and position yourself in the stands until God opens up a hole in the line.

2. Appropriate divine authority.

Almighty God is sending you—under his authority as Lord of the harvest—to influence men and women in his personal harvest field. He gave the seventy authority to overcome all the power of the enemy, and he later gave it to you and me through the Great Commission:

All authority in heaven and on earth has been given to me. Therefore go . . . " (Matthew 28:18-19).

3. Activate a ministry of prayer.

The seventy were told to "Ask the Lord of the harvest, therefore, to send out workers into his harvest field" (Luke 10:2). Need I say anything about the importance of prayer? The Graham team's "Operation Andrew" suggests that you list the names of five or six people that need Christ and start praying for them regularly . . . like every day. As you pray, your courage will grow, your faith will increase, your expectations will multiply. And God will begin to answer your prayers.

Let God construct your prayer list. I would suggest that you ask God to bring to mind a handful of people. Pray about that list for a couple of months. Then list those whom God seems to particularly lay on your heart. Those folks are prime candidates to receive Christ. As you pray, confess your apprehension, acknowledge your fear, and thank him ahead of time for what he is going to do through you and your gifts. That's faith, and faith pleases God.

4. Acknowledge the chariots of fire.

Mental attitude is everything. When you feel discouraged, take a peek at the chariots. When faith wavers, think chariots. When the enemies surround you, remember chariots. When you drive through your neighborhood, walk through those offices, stand in line at the grocery store, think chariots.

5. Assume a new identity.

Who are you? You're a child of the King, a servant of the Lord. A lamb, if you will. Don't despise humility. Pray that the Great Shepherd will enable you to be the least of the saints. Pray that you will pass the apprenticeship to be exalted. Not for your sake, but for his. Living sacrifices are the most powerful people in the world. Bring your gifts on line for service!

6. Assault the enemy.

When you resist the devil, James tells us he must flee from you. Bombard his territory with prayer. Keep the armor on. Stay close to the Shepherd, and Satan can't touch you.

7. Anticipate victory.

"Be sure of this," the Lord told the seventy, "The Kingdom of God is near" (Luke 10:11). A payday is coming, and the Lord assured the seventy that those who rejected them and their message would face severe judgment. Do you remember his words?

> *Woe to you, Korazin! Woe to you, Bethsaida! For if the miracles performed in you had been performed in Tyre and Sidon, they would have repented long ago . . . But it will be more bearable for Tyre and Sidon at the judgment than for you* (Luke 10:13-14).

We'll be vindicated. Our choice to follow him, to turn our back on everything this world holds dear, will be vindicated. All those who rejected us, everyone who spurned the Savior, will one day bow their knees and acknowledge that Jesus is Lord.

The chariots of fire are coming soon, and they're invincible! Nothing will stand against them. We'll step out into eternity with them by the plan and purpose of God.

My friend, that's success with a capital "S." Are you on board?

Eliminate items which hinder effectiveness.

4

PACKING YOUR BAG

When a guy gets to be eight years old, he doesn't have to be hassled anymore. Doesn't need to be mothered. If I liked my clothes on the floor, my dresser drawers open, my bed unmade, what difference was that to them? And this changing of underwear and taking baths stuff—who needed it?

I'd had enough. I was tired of being told what to do. I didn't plan to eat any more broccoli, lima beans, or stewed onions. Enough was enough! Child abuse, that's what it was.

So what could I do about it? Good question. I knew what I'd do. I'd fix them. I'd run away. Yeah, that'd do it. That'd show 'em. Then they'd wish they had me back. Then they'd be sorry for all the grief they'd caused me.

I could just see Mom's face. She'd be crying, pleading. There'd be tears splashing everywhere. Arms outstretched in agony, she'd reach out to her lost son, and he wouldn't be there.

I was feeling better already. I knew what to do. I'd tell her I was leaving. I wouldn't just sneak away. No, I'd tell her. That's it. I'd tell her. That'd teach her. She'd never scold her boy again. He wouldn't be around anymore. She wouldn't send him to bed early, either, or shout at him. Oh, boy! I couldn't wait to see the shock on her face! But I wouldn't give in. No sweet talking or any of that stuff would help her now. It was too late, Mom! Too late. I would tell her—prepare to be shocked!

I told her.

She wasn't.

"So, Joe," she yawned, "when does this little adventure start?"

"Right now," I said fiercely.

"Well, you haven't packed. Why don't you let me help you pack?"

This was unexpected. It wasn't exactly what I had in mind. My lip quivered imperceptibly.

"Go on up to your room," she continued. "I'll get a suitcase."

OK, I would go to my room. But this was the last time. The final trip. I needed some clothes, after all.

"So, how much underwear do you think you'll need? What about t-shirts? Do you want your jammies to sleep in?"

Questions, questions. She kept asking questions. I hated it.

"Shouldn't you take a flashlight? It'll be getting dark soon, you know."

Well, I saw her strategy. It wouldn't work! She couldn't fool me, no sirree! Out the door I went, weighted down with my dad's old suitcase. Dragging it in the dust, I headed north to the swamp. I was mad.

Unfortunately, I was also hungry.

Then twilight came, and worry joined hunger.

When the stars came out, I was done in. Darkness came, darkness conquered.

Soon a humbled little boy headed home. He walked in the door and tried to act like nothing had happened. I tried not to show it too much, but it *was* good to be back. Even the lima beans tasted better.

Packing for the Seventy

The Lord helped the seventy pack. He limited them to flight bags. No excess baggage on this trip. "Do not take a purse or bag or sandals," the Lord told them.

He was tougher on the twelve. "Take nothing for the journey," he said. "No staff, no bag, no bread, no money, no extra tunic" (Luke 9:3).

Something seems odd here. Luke records not more than seventy seconds of our Lord's crucial instructions, and the Spirit instructs him to record the Master's packing requirements? Why include "trivia" in Holy Scriptures? Why include it in both Luke 9 and 10?

Although no reason is given for their inclusion, the prohibitions must have been vital to the success of the mission.

Isn't it interesting that the Lord doesn't tell them what to take, but rather what to leave behind? It is apparently important that certain items be omitted. Jesus must have known that the contraband items would hinder his men's ministry.

Note carefully that the Lord did not ask them to give anything away. He said, "leave it behind."

Could it be that there are times when we, too, must leave some things behind if we are to be redemptive in our relationships? I think so. We carry lots of excess baggage which hinders the mission of Christ. We're most effective when we *take along* certain essentials and *leave behind* certain others.

Effective Evangelism Leaves Security Blankets at Home

Look again at the list of contraband: purses, bags, staffs, sandals, bread, and money. If you've got them, you've got food, clothing, and shelter. The disciples had them. The Lord took them away. Jesus wouldn't let them take food, and they couldn't buy any because he also banned money. Without money, they couldn't stay at an inn. "Leave it behind," said the Lord.

The issue wasn't the possession of extra clothes, food, or money. Rather, it had to do with what would happen to the mission if the disciples trusted in and depended upon their own resources. The fundamental issue seemed to be attitude.

Jesus knew which attitudes make a redemptive person most persuasive and what it takes to facilitate and encourage those attitudes. He also may have been concerned about his disciples' reluctance to associate with unbelievers. He insisted they leave behind those things which would allow them to sustain themselves and thus make it unnecessary to enter pagan households. It was either enter the world of the lost or go hungry.

When you leave behind your MasterCharge, abandon your checking accounts, and forget to take food, you quickly change from being independent to being dependent. It's a change essential to effective persuasion.

In the world of agriculture, pruning and fruit are interrelated. Pruning removes unnecessary or unproductive branches. It's often necessary to prune, to take away something, in order to increase your harvest. When you abundantly possess the necessities of life, you may reach some false conclusions:

"If you've got money, you don't need to trust the Lord. If you've got money, you don't need people."

"If you've got food, you don't need to trust the Lord. If you've got food, you don't need people."

"If you've got plenty of clothes, you don't need to trust the Lord. If you've got clothes, you don't need people."

This simple prohibition placed the seventy into a posture of dependence upon the Lord and upon the people to whom they ministered.

How do you think Amos and Zach felt about it?

"This is going to be great, Amos. Man, let's get this show on the road."

"What's going to be so great about it, Zach?"

"We'll be healing folks and preaching and all that stuff. Besides, think of all the sight-seeing we'll do! You know, I haven't done much traveling."

"Hey, I'm with you! Can't wait to try out my new camera. I'm going to put together a slide show to end all slide shows. I bought twenty-five rolls of film!"

"Amos, don't forget the 'sheep among the wolves' stuff. It won't be a holiday."

"I know that, Zach. That's why I'm glad we've got reservations at a Hilton. If things get rough, we can just retire to the hotel for the day."

"I'm looking forward to that. You know, sleep in a bit, eat a good breakfast . . ."

"And read the paper, sip some coffee."

"Sure! We can do some preaching in the afternoon, and when it gets warm, hit that air conditioned hotel . . ."

"Don't forget the pool, man."

"Tell me about it! How about this? A relaxing dinner at Maxi's, slip into something comfortable, and then-kick back and watch the tube."

Just then, a team captain, Baruch, arrived with some bad news.

"Amos, Zach, you haven't been listening! Jesus just said we couldn't take any money, or food for that matter. We gotta leave it all behind. I suggest you guys cancel those reservations. Sorry about that."

The news hit hard.

"Did you hear that, Zach, what the Lord said? Why would he say something like that? It doesn't make sense to me!"

But it does make sense. Anything that encourages us to be independent of God or man is bound to get us in trouble. When you hit town with nothing, with nowhere to stay, nothing to eat, and no extra suit of clothes, you'll pray and trust. Furthermore, your focus will be on people and relationships, not on events and programs. It will be personal, not impersonal.

Effective Evangelism Abandons Pretense

As we're stripped of outward evidences of success, we're open and vulnerable to those people we are reaching for Christ. We're not overcome by status anxieties and bleeding ulcers. We may be successful, but it's not our trump card. We could "win," but we choose not to. We make that decision as part of an effective strategy. People who know this say things like:

"I'm a dependent person because I left my wallet home."

"I'm a grateful person because someone else is providing food."

"I'm a thankful person because someone is providing shelter."

"I'm a helpful person because someone is helping me."

With that mindset, I am most powerful for God. The alternative? To view myself as some sort of spiritual Bwana. Clothed in khaki shorts, white shirt, and pith helmet, I charge out into the neighborhood, six inches off the ground, to win it for Christ. All the while I'm "looking down on them to save them." Ugh.

We're not called to shout the good news from a safe and respectable distance and then leave. To reach men and women for Christ, we must voluntarily lay aside the temptation to be detached from the unsaved or to lord it over them.

As the disciples thought through the implications of the Lord's restrictions, "attitude adjustment hour" hit. Effective service, it seems, is much more attitude than aptitude. It's pretty humbling to have to depend on others.

Effective Evangelism Abandons Worldly Patterns of Persuasion

Do you want to effectively reach your friends and neighbors for Christ? Jesus has some guidelines.

No power suits allowed. Leave behind your Rolaids, your Rolex, your Rolls and your bank roll. Power, position, and possessions are not the tools of the trade for a redemptive person.

The issue is not that you possess such things, but that you'll be tempted to use them inappropriately. Obviously, achievement is recognized and appreciated. And God *can* use it. Our trust in it as a tool of persuasion, however, is wrong.

It's not necessary to spice up genuine faith with any of this world's condiments. If you've got the disease of carnality, people know it. A carnal Christian can be buried under this world's success symbols and still stink.

The Bible calls us clay pots which contain a treasure. The treasure, of course, is Christ. Lifestyle evangelism is not an attempt to decorate and shine the pot; folks need to see the treasure, not the container. Only a broken container lets the radiance of the treasure penetrate the darkness.

In our brokenness, we're called to be redemptive people. Sheep are most powerful when they're aware of their absolute vulnerability. If Christ (not our position, power, and possessions) is lifted up, he will draw all men unto himself.

Effective Evangelism Forfeits the Right to Control Circumstances

Money represents power. With it I can gain a measure of independence. I can stay where I want, eat what I choose, wear what pleases me, and impress others. I can also ignore what I want. That's what's dangerous about being self-sufficient.

"Leave it home," the Lord said. When Amos and Zach hit town, their agenda was largely determined by the beneficence of others. They couldn't demand or buy shelter, and it was highly unlikely God would turn stones into food for them. No, they had to humble themselves and ask for help. Dynamite!

Part of long-term persuasion is to let others set the

agenda. We must abandon the need to control, to possess, and to dominate. Ultimately, we trust that God's agenda will prevail. "Not my will, but thine be done," is the prayer we echo. Natural and spiritual babies have a way of arriving at the most inconvenient times. It's seldom convenient to cultivate, sow, or reap. The wolf sees to that.

Effective Evangelism Doesn't Tell God How He Must Work

God is a God of surprises. His ways aren't ours. Often, the worst methods are the customary methods. All who are to be saved must come to the foot of the Cross, but few get there the same way. There are myriad ways to Calvary. As a general rule, God blesses men, not methods. Methods are tools which produce results when utilized by godly men.

Dr. T. J. Bach, one of the greatest missionary statesmen of a previous generation, found Christ through a tract. When a stranger handed him the tract on the streets of Chicago, he immediately tore it up and threw it on the street. Tears started coursing down the cheeks of the stranger. Strangely touched, Dr. Bach stooped over, picked up the pieces, and put them in his pocket. Returning to his room, he reassembled the tract, read it, and received Christ as his Savior.

Lifestyle evangelism is a way of living, not a method. In Bach's case, the tears said it all . . . in a matter of seconds. It was a broken heart that stopped Dr. Bach in his tracks. The tract, coupled with the man, proved to be an effective method.

Remember that Paul could say, "I have become all things to all men, so *that by all possible means* I might win some." God works through football games, fishing trips, barbecues, and Billy Graham. He often hands souls from one person to another until the time is right for that individual to respond. Countless thousands have "handed off souls" to those whose reaping gifts God uses to "give the increase."

Effective Evangelism Avoids Gimmicks and Gismos

Forget the gospel pencils and erasers, the bumper stickers, the gospel blimps. They are not in the mainstream of God's redemptive strategy. To reach a lost person is a difficult, time consuming, costly struggle. When things get tough, it's always good to stick to the basics of loving, caring, and serving in the name of Christ. That behavior produces a light which can burn through hardened steel. Peter had exactly this in mind when he wrote:

> *Above all, love each other deeply, because love covers over a multitude of sins. Offer hospitality to one another without grumbling. Each one should use whatever gift he has received to serve others, faithfully administering God's grace in its various forms. If anyone speaks, he should do it as one speaking the very words of God. If anyone serves, he should do it with the strength God provides, so that in all things God may be praised through Jesus Christ* (1 Peter 4:8-11).

Don't be fooled by imitations. Many who think they have harnessed the Holy Spirit have simply harnessed cheap psychology and slick tricks of persuasion. Genuine soul-winning is not plastic or easy. The Lord referred to

it as "hard labor." But don't forget that the seventy returned with joy!

Effective Evangelism Communicates the Gospel

The "health and wealth" gospel boys would have been
greatly offended by our Lord's instructions to "leave it all
behind, keep it out of sight." Of course, if God wants
everyone healthy and wealthy, it makes sense that he
give them visual aids to trumpet the truth of their claims.
But Jesus said, "Leave them behind." I wonder what
would happen to the silk suits, diamond studs, Rolex
watches, and Cadillacs if the health and wealth crowd
followed Christ's instructions?

I guess the poor boys in Hebrews 11 missed it, too.
They trusted Christ and ended up in chains. They were
beaten, hunted like animals, hacked to pieces. Fugitives
with a bounty on their heads, they lived in caves and
dens. Destitute, poverty-stricken, desperate, God said
they were so incredibly special that the world was not
worthy of them. But somehow, it seems, they missed it.
They never "moved on up."

It is true that God, in his goodness, blesses some of
his children with material things. But health and wealth
is not the "manifest destiny" of every believer.

The gospel isn't prime rib on every platter or a Cadillac
in every garage. The gospel is the good news of Christ's
victory. It is the good news that God's forgiving, healing,
and restoring power is available to overcome the disrup-
tive, destructive, engulfing power of sin. Now, that's good
news! Evangelism is simply the introduction of this healing and restoring power into webs of human relationships.
Faith in Jesus Christ makes this healing and restoring
power available to everyone.

Effective Evangelism Abandons
Inappropriate Methodologies

The Great Commission provides a standard for evaluating methodologies. "Therefore go" our Lord said, "and make *disciples* of all nations . . ." Notice that it does not say "Go, and *decision* all nations." The responsibility of the biblical evangelist goes far beyond leading a person to Christ. The task of evangelism involves bringing people to a point of discipleship. We want full-term babies. Logic suggests that our methodology be influenced by those factors which produce disciples of Christ. How would the following facts (some of which you've already seen) influence your understanding and approach to evangelism?

- More than 80 percent of those who trust Christ and remain members of a local church are led to the Lord by a friend. Furthermore, they have had over five (5.9) exposures to the gospel before their conversion.

- More than 70 percent of those who "trust Christ" and drop out of the church are led to the Lord by a stranger. These converts average a little over two exposures (2.16) to the gospel before their conversion.

- Seventy percent of those who remain as members of a local church were led to Christ by someone who viewed evangelism as a non-manipulative dialogue. Almost 90 percent of those who "drop out" were led to Christ by someone who perceived evangelism as a manipulative dialogue.

- Those who remain as members of a local church had developed significant contacts with church members before their conversion.

- Those who continue in the church have established significant friendships within the church following their conversion.

- More than 90 percent of those who remain within the fellowship of the church following conversion were dissatisfied with their non-religious lifestyle before anyone proclaimed the gospel to them. More than 75 percent of those who "drop out" of the fellowship following conversion showed no significant level of dissatisfaction before conversion.

If our goal is to "decision" all nations and our neighbors, then our methodology doesn't much matter. If we, however, are to help them become disciples of Christ, our methods become critically important.

A mature believer has progressed through three important levels. He has made a commitment to Christ, to the church, and to God's purposes in this world. Whatever strategy we adopt, it should contain whatever dynamics are necessary to bring the lost to Christ, fold them into a local fellowship of believers, and deploy them into the world as redemptive people. Anything short of that is truncated.

As we think of methodology, we are looking at networks. We're thinking of those clusters of people linked around a common cause or location. How are you going to best influence those with whom you are in regular contact—the gang at the office, the ladies in the baby-sitting co-op, the parents and players on the team, those folks in your neighborhood, the PTA, your hunting buddies?

The Lord's mandate to disciple all nations, plus the above data, forces us to acknowledge that a lifestyle of openness and personal involvement is the critical factor in becoming a fully redemptive person. That's why evangelism is fundamentally a way of living which utilizes methods appropriate to the target audience.

Effective Evangelism Maintains a Believer's Stature

Does this sound contrary to what I said earlier? It's not. Redemptive people are not lepers or second-class citizens. We go out with a humble spirit and graciously accept the assistance and help of others. We go with a willingness to offer the gift of our need when it is appropriate. But we do not go tail-between- our-legs, feeling inferior and abused.

Yes, some challenging dynamics were introduced to Mission Seventy when Amos and the troops had to leave behind some of their things. But the Lord affirmed the value of what they did when he said, "the worker deserves his wages" (Luke 10:7). Workers get paid for a product or a service. The Lord suggested that any costs their hosts would incur would be amply reimbursed by the benefits introduced through the gospel. When we offer the love and forgiveness of Christ, we offer the most precious commodity in the world. Our attitude of dependence is balanced by an awareness of the magnitude of what we give.

Effective Evangelism Requires a New Wardrobe

The seventy were limited to one set of clothes, but they were clothed. The Lord didn't tell them what to take, but obviously they took the essentials. This stripped-down wardrobe made their essential character much more visible. The things which count showed through!

In Matthew 5, the Lord describes a salty torchbearer. In the imagery of salt and light, he warns against loss of flavor and loss of visibility. Like salt, we impart flavor; like light, we reveal character. The immediate context describes eight qualities of a God-flavored person:

Blessed are the poor in spirit.

Blessed are those who mourn.

Blessed are the meek.

Blessed are those who hunger and thirst after righteousness.

Blessed are the merciful.

Blessed are the pure in heart.

Blessed are the peacemakers.

Blessed are those who are persecuted because of righteousness.

YOU ARE THE SALT OF THE EARTH . . .
YOU ARE THE LIGHT OF THE WORLD . . .
(Matthew 5:3-14).

Who is?

Those who:

. . . are poor in spirit

. . . mourn

. . . are meek

. . . hunger and thirst for righteousness

. . . are merciful

. . . are pure

. . . are peacemakers

. . . are persecuted because of righteousness

Read the list again. It speaks for itself. What's missing from the list? The proud, the pushy, the arrogant. The impure, the tainted, the cruel. The contentious, the divisive, the inconsiderate.

Isn't this list describing a godly servant? This person thirsts for righteousness and purity. He is meek, merciful, and a peacemaker. Interesting, isn't it, that the Beatitudes are immediately followed by a discussion about our role as salt and light. "Let your light so shine before men that they may see your good deeds," performed with an attitude of meekness, gentleness, purity, righteousness, mercy, and peace.

Effective Evangelism Requires a New Identity

We've already discussed this at some length. We're sheep. Attack lambs, if you please. Our greatest weapon? Love and service in the name of Christ. We leave behind our designer jeans and clothe ourselves with the beatitudes, with the fruit of the spirit. We do not consider the non-Christian our enemy. We do not see ourselves as superior to the lost. As towel wearers and basin bearers, we look up to them to serve them.

In Matthew's parallel passage to Luke 10, the Lord uses an animal, a bird, and a snake to help round out the seventy's identity. He sends them out as lambs with instructions to "be as shrewd as snakes and as innocent as doves" (Matthew 10:16). The word *shrewd* comes from the Greek root meaning "mind." It suggests that we be intelligent, alert, and use common sense. Meekness and gentleness are not to be confused with being stupid or gullible. We're not to be dumb sheep, just sheep. The "shrewdness" is to be balanced by acquiring the innocence and purity of a dove.

We've already seen Paul's shrewdness as highlighted in 1 Corinthians 9:20 ff., but it wouldn't hurt to look at it again. He writes:

To the Jews, I became like a Jew to win the Jews. To those under the law I became like one under the law, so as to win those under the law.

To those not having the law, I became like one not having the law, so as to win those not having the law. To the weak I became weak, to win the weak.

I have become all things to all men so that by all possible means I might save some.

It almost looks like the identity he assumes is as important as the message he communicates. Certainly, the two are vitally linked. It's common sense to take an interest in people and their world if you want them to take an interest in you and yours. In Paul's thinking, to win a newspaperman, you become like a newspaperman.

Davis was an executive with the *Dallas Morning News*. One day I said, "Davis, I'd love to come down to your office and have you show me what happens from the time something comes in on the wire until the newspaper hits the pavement." I wanted to go to his turf and take an interest in that which interested him.

Davis was excited that I wanted to "become a newspaperman." He showed me everything. We spent the morning looking at the editorial department, copy writers, typesetting machines, and the paper's mammoth, two-story press. He took me to lunch at the Petroleum Club. I learned a lot, and enjoyed the experience.

Soon after, Davis committed his life to Christ. Because I took an interest in his world, he took an interest in mine. By letting him share his world from a position of strength, he was willing to share the weakness of his unseen world.

Effective Evangelism Utilizes Divine Dynamics

It is God who gives the increase. His Spirit convicts of sin, righteousness, and judgment. He opens doors, provides food and clothing, and enables us to assume an identity with persuasive power. It is the Holy Spirit who is the real midwife to a newly-born soul.

The Lord's travel restrictions reduced his followers to a position of total dependence and trust. Have you ever met a well-meaning, fervent young businessman whose goal is to make a fortune by the time he's thirty-five, retire, and serve the Lord without depending upon anyone? As a general rule, I don't believe that dream comes from God.

The Lord didn't ask the seventy to give away their money or sell their suits at a garage sale. He said to leave behind everything which would tempt them to trust anything but him.

It's a hard lesson to learn, but a crucial one. Even Amos and Zach finally learned it.

"Well, Zach, I guess we're here. Doesn't look like the village has changed much."

"That's true, Amos, but look at the new Hilton! It's a pretty posh place. Which reminds me—where are we staying?"

"Not there, that's for sure."

"Don't you think we'd better start punching some door bells? We might find someone who'd put us up for the night."

"Sounds like a winner to me. It's not getting any earlier."

And so they went, door to door, stranger to stranger.

"Shalom, friend! I'm Zach, and this is my friend, Amos. We're followers of Jesus of Nazareth."

SLAM!

"Hey, Amos, I thought the Lord said the fields were ripe unto harvest. These folks are downright hostile. I don't know about this plan, Amos old buddy. That's the fifth house!"

"Yeah, I know. He wasn't kidding about the wolves. I'm ready for a hot shower and a good meal."

"Dream on, friend. Hey, let's try one more. Amos, push the button."

Ring!

"Hello! I'm Zach, and this is my friend, Amos. We're disciples of Jesus from Nazareth. You know, the one who's been doing all the miracles and holding class outdoors? You've heard of him?"

They had, they were interested, they invited in our weary pair, and they provided food and shelter. Zach and Amos spoke not only of the good news of Christ, but gave the gift of their need.

Likewise, Christ offered the gift of his need to the Samaritan woman when he could have snapped his fingers and materialized an ice-cold RC. How desperately she needed affirmation! Have you ever realized that one of the greatest gifts you can present is the gift of your need? Think about it. What does that posture do to help build a redemptive relationship? Think how affirming it is to have someone share a need with you!

We err in thinking that God sends us out as paragons of strength. We err in thinking we witness by showing off our adequacy. We err when we give our testimony as a continuous story of success and victory. We err when we suggest we don't need anyone else, especially unbelievers. We err when we think being dependent is to be weak, or that failure disqualifies us from evangelism, or that worldly patterns of persuasion are necessary.

We do right when we admit our need and depend on Christ's provision, in whatever form it comes.

Effective Evangelism Uses What's in Your Own Sack

Look inside your sack. God can use whatever's in it. He can feed five thousand with your gifts and abilities. Paul told Timothy to "stir up his gift." Most tools need sharpening, adjusting, or repair of some kind. God wants us to develop and use what he has given us; he doesn't want us clamoring after someone else's gift. If we desire to reach people, God will provide the opportunity.

A man new to the neighborhood was mowing his lawn with an ancient handpush lawnmower. Across the street, a Christian neighbor was watching. He'd been praying for a way to reach his new friend for Christ, and when he saw the struggle with the antiquated grass gasher, a light bulb went on. There was a brand new power mower in his sack!

He wheeled it across the street and insisted that his new neighbor use it—not just that day, but every time the grass needed mowing.

About eight weeks later, there was a knock at the door, and there stood the new neighbor, Bible in hand. Not an ordinary Bible, mind you. This was one of those monster, twenty-seven-pound Family Bibles. "This is a Bible," his friend announced.

Yes, it certainly was. Rather awkwardly, the man pointed out his family tree, the marriage certificates at the front, and the burial notices. Finally, he asked, "How can I be born again?" My Christian friend had the privilege of pointing his neighbor to Christ . . . because of a lawnmower. Like I say, use what you have, and do it deliberately!

Effective Evangelism Avoids All Hindrances

"Don't greet anyone on the way," the Lord told the seventy. That comment poses some problems for a guy writing a book on friendship evangelism.

Right away, we note that there's no textual problem. It means exactly what it says. So what did Jesus have in mind?

Remember that the Lord had clearly defined the mission. He told his men where to go and what to do. Now he's telling them not to get involved in anything which might detract from the mission, good as those things may be. It's *the principle of priority.*

Paul abandoned all kinds of rights so that he wouldn't scuttle the mission. So must we.

The commission of God which comes upon every believer must be given highest priority. That means we put top value upon God's agenda for our lives. Other values, as good as they may be, play second banana to the gospel mission.

There's nothing wrong about chatting with folks along the road . . . unless it keeps you from reaching your town for Christ.

Remember, the lost are blind and deceived.

5

FINDING THE LOST SHEEP

Diploma in hand, he signed on as a farmer. Now a graduate of Aggie Tech, he was ready to follow in the tradition of his grand alma mater. He decided to grow chickens. Cranking up the John Deere, he headed out to the fields to plow, disc, and harrow. Finally he planted his chickens head first in rows.

They didn't do too well; in fact, they all expired within minutes. But the Aggie wasn't one to give up easily, so he fired up the old John Deere and doggedly prepared the soil for a second batch, this time planting the birds feet first. To his credit, this crop kicked up dust for a little longer, but they, too, soon kicked the bucket.

Failure was staring him in the face. Something was wrong! But what? Suddenly it dawned on him that as an alumnus of Aggie Tech, he could write the extension department, describe his problem, and get a solution. With renewed hope, he sat down at the kitchen table with its purple formica top and chrome legs and put his problems on paper. He finished his letter, addressed it, sealed it, popped it in the mailbox, and put up the red flag.

Days later, a letter came addressed to him from "Aggie Tech: Extension Division." At last, he had his answer!

Hustling into the kitchen, he slashed open the envelope and yanked out the note. It was short.

"Dear sir: Please send soil sample."

Give the boy credit. He worked hard for a crop; he just didn't know much about chickens.

In modified biblical terms, the boy was innocent as a dove, but shrewd as a tomato. His intelligence lagged way behind his enthusiasm.

When the Lord deployed the twelve and the seventy, he, too, expected fruit. In one of his teaching parables, he spoke plainly about unproductive plants. Luke 13 records these words:

> A man had a fig tree, planted in his vineyard, and he went to look for fruit on it, but did not find any. So he said to the man who took care of the vineyard, "For three years now I've been coming to look for fruit on this fig tree and haven't found any. Cut it down! Why should it use up the soil?"

> "Sir," the man replied, "leave it alone for one more year, and I'll dig around it and fertilize it. If it bears fruit next year, fine! If not, then cut it down" (Luke 13:6-9).

The story ends without telling us what happened to the tree. The worker obviously was emotionally attached to it. He tried to spare the tree by offering to cultivate it and fertilize it so that it might yield a bountiful harvest. The farmer's interest was fruit; the tree was simply a means to produce it. If it was barren, why let it deplete the soil? If it was dying, bury it.

The farmer certainly had a pragmatic approach to agriculture. "If there's no fruit, cut it down. Leaves aren't enough."

I wonder what would happen if we applied this same principle to many of our approaches to evangelism?

God has already provided us with much to assure our fruitfulness. He's provided us with a strategy and case studies to show us how it works. He's peeled back the curtain to let us see the abundant harvest and the chariots of fire. He's scouted the opposition and given us insights into their attack. He's tagged us as lambs and has helped us see the power of vulnerability. He's established travel restrictions to teach dependence and gratitude. He's placed various gifts in our lunch sacks to equip us for unique ministries.

So with all this backing us up, do we feel ready to flow into a web of relationships and network them for Christ?

"I'm not sure, Joe," you say. "I feel inadequate, and I don't know much about non-Christians. I wouldn't know where to begin."

You sound pretty normal to me! Let's talk about these things.

What Are Lost Sheep Like?

"Go to the lost sheep of Israel," the Lord told the twelve (Matthew 10:6). Notice that he sent them to a very specific audience. They were to focus upon Jews, not Gentiles—lost Jews who were like sheep. What is a lost sheep like? It's a crucial question, because the more we understand our lost friends, the better we will be able to explain the gospel.

1. Our unsaved friends are lost.

Apart from a new birth, our non-Christian friends are doomed to everlasting darkness. They are like sheep without a shepherd. The word *lost* comes from a root word which means "ruined" or "destroyed." It is used of wine that has lost its flavor and sheep that have gone astray. The father of the prodigal son exclaimed, "This my son was lost, and is found." Because they are lost, we should

... not expect regenerate behavior from them

... accept them in their lostness

... expect actions in keeping with their nature

... plead with God for their salvation

... pray that our hearts will be moved by their lostness

2. They are spiritually dead.

Paul said the unsaved were "dead in trespasses and sin" (Ephesians 2:1). He said they are "alienated from God" and are his "enemies" (Colossians 1:21). He wrote that "the god of this age has blinded the minds of unbelievers, so that they cannot see the light of the gospel of the glory of Christ," and further explained that they are blind to the glory of God revealed in the face of Christ (2 Corinthians 4:4-6).

Being spiritually dead does not mean the lost cannot repeat the "words" of the gospel. Notice that it is their *minds* that are dysfunctional. The gospel doesn't seem appropriate to them. They don't think they need it. Without God, they have a "God-shaped vacuum" which they are trying to fill with material pleasures and toys. Because they are spiritually dead, we should

... not expect to see signs of life

... expect they would misunderstand the gospel

... live the gospel before them

... cultivate the parched soil of their souls

3. Their emotions are degraded.

This doesn't mean every non-Christian has gone the whole way down the wrong emotional road. Many are quite moral and upright by society's standards. Yet most struggle with such works of the flesh as hatred, discord, jealousy, selfish ambition, envy, etc. Many struggle with sexual temptation and unfaithfulness. Some are into pornography and other perversions. Many are desperate for help in building healthy relationships. Because of their emotional disabilities, we should

. . . anticipate conflict

. . . expect to uncover relationship problems

. . . expect to be propositioned

. . . model commitment and faithfulness

4. They are intellectually handicapped.

Paul spoke of this in Romans 1:22 where, speaking of the unsaved, he wrote "Although they claimed to be wise, they became fools." God gave them over to a depraved mind. They considered the things of God foolish and were incapable of understanding them without divine help (1 Corinthians 2:14). That's still true today. Most do not have a thoughtfully considered world view. Because of Satanic blindness, we should

. . . expect intellectual confusion

. . . anticipate they will reject our ideas as intellectually absurd

. . . know something of a biblical world view

. . . not expect intellectual debate to be effective

5. *Many are socially disillusioned.*

Captured by the evil ways of this age, they have climbed aboard the hedonistic bandwagon. Commitment and intimacy are mysteries to many of them. Highly mobile, it is not unusual for them to flit from one relationship to another. Divorce has touched most. A growing number are victims of sexual abuse. In many cases, the family unit is being torn apart. Few have deep friendships.

These social and marital pressures provide open doors for the gospel. Folks who are not yet interested in saving their souls may be interested in learning how to save their marriages and families. Just discovering a good friend may nudge them in that direction. To reach them, we should

- . . . be consistent and trustworthy in our relationships
- . . . affirm them as valuable people
- . . . expect them to be difficult to get close to
- . ... become a friend
- . . . plan on listening to lots of pain and hurt
- . . . begin with felt needs

6. *Some are economically deceived.*

Many believe the key to happiness is grabbing possessions, position, and power. Some have achieved the "big three" and suffer from destination sickness. They've climbed the ladder and now wonder if it's leaning against the wrong wall.

When the seed of the gospel comes, many miss it because "the worries of this life and the deceitfulness of wealth choke it, making it unfruitful" (Matthew 13:22). These folks are open to observing a nonmaterialistic

Christian or couple enjoy an abundant life through Christ. To help them we should

- . . . model a lifestyle which derives its satisfaction from God
- . . . not be caught up in the materialistic rat race
- . . . show them love
- . . . plan good times around simple, inexpensive activities
- . . . be a gracious recipient of their kindness

7. Some are economically disadvantaged.

Many people need to experience the love of Christ in tangible ways. They need help, not a hand-out—help without strings attached. Pounding nails, fixing roofs, mending fences, and replacing fuse boxes are ways we can show the love of Christ in practical ways. To respond as light, we should

- . . . let our actions speak as loud as our words
- . . . anticipate the difficulty they will have in accepting help
- . . . discover ways to affirm their value and worth
- . . . include them in social activities
- . . . network them with social agencies which provide help
- . . . protect their dignity

8. Some are physically unfocused.

Whether living a life of sensuality or worshiping at the health spa, ultimately these folks will grow dissatisfied with both options. Gravity eventually wins. Aging cannot be reversed. Multiple sexual encounters dilute the soul, and many have been hurt through such abuse of their sexuality. A physical focus can never satisfy the deep longings of the heart. To assist them we should

. . . be responsible stewards of our own bodies

. . . exercise with them

. . . model faithfulness

. . . withstand temptation

. . . be available to listen

9. Most are religiously unsophisticated.

The lost tend to be ecumenical in their approach to man and God, opposing sectarianism or any other claim to religious exclusivity. Some are in open rebellion against God, while others consider him irrelevant. Many would consider Christianity narrow and rigid. The religions of the East have a growing appeal.

None of them want to be a project. Most have not rejected Christ, but a caricature of him. If he is exalted through the life of a friend, the unbeliever will pay attention. To help them we should

. . . not bury them under theological insight

. . . let them explain their beliefs first,
        without attacking them

. . . ask questions

. . . be gentle, refusing to argue

. . . live our faith through practical love
        and service

10. *Many are suspicious and skeptical.*

Most unbelievers are convinced that Christians can smell sin on them . . . and sometimes you can. They tend to be wary of impersonal approaches to the gospel. Some have been burned by unfortunate evangelism efforts; they've been "evangelized" and dumped. To help them, we should

. . . be accepting and loving

. . . be slow to speak

. . . be genuine in our friendship

. . . be sympathetic to their negative experiences

. . . ask questions

. . . reflect godly motives

. . . be sensitive to signs of readiness

. . . be slow to judge

11. *They are vulnerable to love.*

No doubt there are more wrong approaches than there are resistant folks, but you can't go wrong by loving them. In fact, we're commanded to do just that. As I've said, we're not commanded to evangelize them, just love them. If we really do love them, however, we will evangelize them.

The apostle John tells us that "love is made complete among us so that we will have confidence on the day of judgment . . . perfect love drives out fear, because fear has to do with punishment" (1 John 4:17-18). If we love someone, we want to do whatever is necessary to eliminate fear, especially the fear of judgment and punishment. Knowing that "as man is destined to die once, and after that to face judgment" (Hebrews 9:27), we are compelled to share the gospel. It is a fearful thing to be judged by a holy God.

The loving thing to do is to proclaim the good news that Christ did everything necessary to bear our punishment, and that by trusting him we can have peace with God. Because love is so potent, we should

   . . . love, love, love

   . . . look for opportunities to serve

   . . . look for opportunities to give

   . . . allow our lost friends to give and serve

12. *The lost vary in their receptivity.*

Some unbelievers will be downright hostile, others will be interested, a few will be open. There will be cultural, social, economic, political, racial, and religious barriers to overcome. The more barriers there are to bridge, the more difficult the challenge. Generally, those who are most like you will be be the easiest to reach. Because of this great diversity, we should

   . . . become aware of these barriers

   . . . plan a strategy which minimizes the barriers

   . . . establish a profile of those who would be most receptive

   . . . capitalize on a believer's distinctive differences

   . . . become naturalized citizens of their world

   . . . recognize some will reject us

These are some beginning thoughts on the kind of people you'll be contacting as you seek to become a redemptive person. But how do you find these lost sheep?

Jesus' Evangelistic Game Plan

The disciples were sent out instructed to search diligently for a certain kind of person. They were not to try a hit and miss approach. Observe our Lord's instructions to the "dazzlin' dozen:"

> *Whatever town or village you enter, search for some worthy person there and stay at his house until you leave. As you enter the home, give it your greeting. If the home is deserving, let your peace rest on it; if not, let your peace return to you* (Matthew 10:11-13).

The word *search* implies a strict examination. It is used of being questioned in a courtroom. Herod sent the Magi to Bethlehem and told them to "Go and make a careful *search* for the child" (Matthew 2:8).

The principle of focusing ministry on a particular audience is taught in the Sermon on the Mount. With strong language, our Lord said

> *Do not give dogs what is sacred; do not throw your pearls to pigs. If you do, they may trample them under their feet, and then turn and tear you to pieces* (Matthew 7:6).

For economy of effort and to get the greatest return on your investment of time and energy, you must discern whom you can and cannot influence for Christ. Dogs have no awareness or appreciation for what is sacred. Pigs are incapable of discerning the value of pearls. The prohibitions are clear: Do not give dogs sacred things. Do not give pigs anything valuable.

Barking dogs and squealing pigs are easily recognized. How do you recognize human "dogs" and "pigs?" Three clues are given:

1. Their frame of reference is secular, not sacred. They have no interest or awareness of that which is religious, sacred, or spiritual.

2. They are insensitive to that which is of value.

3. They are dangerous.

The Lord's terminology of dogs and pigs is not accidental. In biblical times, the dog was considered an "unclean" animal. Packs of wild dogs roamed the streets, feeding upon garbage and other refuse. They were considered the lowest form of vileness.

To be called a "dog" was to be labeled an impure, profane, or despised person. The Jews called Gentiles "dogs." Likewise, Paul refers to false apostles as "dogs" in Philippians 3:2. Jesus is not instructing the disciples to avoid those who are ignorant of sacred things; he is talking about those who are impure, profane, and contemptuous of sacred things.

Both Jews and Moslems loathe swine. Pigs are symbols of the despicable and the vile. The ultimate act of spiritual treason was to offer a pig on a Jewish altar. So brutish are such creatures that they stamp priceless things into the mud, then turn on those trying to help them. The danger comes from a fully matured, adult swine, not a baby one.

The Lord is instructing his disciples to avoid giving that which is priceless and beautiful to brutes. The prohibitions set up by the Lord do not mean that "dogs" and "pigs" are beyond salvation. As long as they are in full rebellion against sacred and valuable things, however, it is not wise for Christians to proclaim the Good News to them. Even so, this does not preclude the Spirit working in their hearts.

Summing It Up

As we consider becoming allied with a network of people that we hope to impact for Christ, there are several principles to observe.

1. Some unbelievers will be in active rebellion against the sacred and the valuable.

2. Some will be dangerous. It takes a high degree of spiritual maturity and biblical knowledge to deal with those hardened in sin and rebellion. It may not be wise for you to expose yourself or your family to such people.

3. Some will be receptive. The Lord successfully deployed his disciples to locate worthy men and worthy homes.

4. We will be much more effective in evangelism when we develop our ability to detect "readiness."

5. The gospel is sacred and must be communicated and received for what it is.

6. All souls are vulnerable to prayer.

7. The same message of Christ planted in several places will not yield the same results.

Getting Prepared for Contact

We've seen that lambs against the wolf pack are greatly disadvantaged. If we only thought about the task God gave us, and forgot about the power he's promised, we'd all either give up or fall apart.

The solution to this dilemma is our Shepherd. He has authority over all the forces that oppose us. To have authority is to have the right "to control, command, or determine." That authority, my friend, has been delegated to you and me. It is ours to appropriate. Remember what Matthew wrote?

> *He called his twelve disciples to him and gave them authority to drive out evil spirits and to heal every disease and sickness.*
>
> *"Be on your guard against men; they will hand you over to the local councils and flog you in their synagogues. On my account you will be brought before governors and kings as witnesses to them and to the Gentiles. But when they arrest you, do not worry about what to say or how to say it. At that time you will be given what to say, for it will not be you speaking, but the Spirit of your Father speaking through you."* (Matthew 10:1, 17-20).

Jesus told the seventy:

> *I have given you authority . . . to overcome all the power of the enemy; nothing will harm you* (Luke 10:19).

He tells you and me:

> *All authority in heaven and on earth has been given to me. Therefore go and make disciples of all nations. . .* (Matthew 28:18-19).
>
> *But you will receive power when the Holy Spirit comes on you; and you will be my witnesses. . .* (Acts 1:8).

Notice several significant verbs: "to drive out," "to heal," "to overcome," "to go," "to make disciples," and "to be witnesses."

God will supply whatever it takes to do the things he requires. The words *power* and *authority* tell us that God enables those who move out in obedience to his commission.

So what holds us back? I can think of several reasons.

1. We are not used to power.

Our involvement with church activities seldom requires power. In fact, it is possible our sometimes "neurotic Christian activism" is actually an escape mechanism, for we feel powerless to contribute to those who are in desperate need. In many churches, the problem is not so much a power "failure" as its absence altogether. In some cases, claims of God's power turn out to be greatly distorted.

2. We lack power because of unbelief.

Let's face it, our actions are always the products of our true convictions. Seldom, if ever, do action and conviction contradict each other. You act on what you truly believe. If my actions differ from what the Bible teaches, it's because I don't believe what the Bible teaches, no matter how loudly I protest that I do. The bottom line is unbelief.

Fortunately, not everyone has fallen into the unbelief mode. I frequently speak at a wonderful church in Eugene, Oregon, which has a goal to plant one hundred churches in the next few years. Thirty-five neighboring towns already have been identified as needing churches. In this church's seven years of existence, it has purchased a seventeen-acre site, built a sixteen-hundred-seat auditorium, assembled a congregation of fifteen hundred, and already planted seven churches.

The pastoral staff takes one service a month to review the church's vision with its people. Do I need to say that it's an "alive" church? Its goal is to see eight hundred trust the Lord through its ministry during the calendar year.

3. We expect power before we need it.

When God's will becomes clear, we mistakenly expect to receive his power immediately. But God's power is provided when it is needed, not in advance. That's what's scary about faith.

Many seldom experience the power of God because they avoid situations where they might need it. The Holy Spirit could drop out of many churches for a month and not be missed.

We are called to be obedient to the heavenly vision. The biblical pattern is that we respond to his commission, expecting enablement when it's needed. That's faith.

We don't test God's resources until we attempt the impossible. We insult God when we tell him of our inadequacy and then ask if we might therefore be excused. It's accusing him of shoddy workmanship. The only way a "nobody" could exist would be for God to make such a person, and he never did so. He never made a nobody.

4. We expect power before we're qualified for it.

God does not pour out his blessing indiscriminately. Spiritual clout is both a victory and a gift. Power and purity of life are twin sisters; you can't have one without the other. Some want more power when it is purity they need.

Powerful people are the meek who hunger and thirst after righteousness. Their deepest motivation is to please the Lord, and they've learned to walk in step with the Spirit of God.

Other folks live godly lives, yet never penetrate the non-Christian world. They trust God for godliness, but not for usefulness and effectiveness in accomplishing their redemptive mission. Redemptive people need God's enablement to:

. . . grow in Christ

. . . overcome the lusts of the flesh

. . . produce the fruits of the spirit

. . . resist the evil one

. . . build redemptive relationships

. . . avoid compromise

. . . overcome the fear of rejection

. . . talk about God

. . . serve the needs of others

. . . initiate and maintain contact with unbelievers

. . . find responsive unbelievers

. . . establish adequate priorities

. . . maintain a balance between being and doing

. . . conquer fear

. . . love non-Christians

Whenever we're involved in a faith enterprise, we're overextended by divine design. That's what faith is all about. It's a response of obedience to an impossible request. It's inviting five thousand friends to sit down for a meal prepared from the meager contents of a hungry lad's lunch sack. Don't you think it would've been a lot easier if the Lord had first created a big mound of loaves and fish, then said,

"OK boys, what do you think we ought to serve for supper?"

"How 'bout fish sandwiches?"

"Great idea! Seat 'em and serve 'em."

It might have been a lot easier, but that's not what

most pleased God. Enablement extends to those difficult situations when we don't know what to do or say:

> "At that time," Jesus said, "you will be given what to say, for it will not be you speaking, but the Spirit of your Father speaking through you" (Matthew 10:19-20).

Does that mean it's just in the difficult times that God speaks through us? Listen to Paul:

> We are therefore Christ's ambassadors, as though God were making his appeal through us. We implore you on Christ's behalf: Be reconciled to God (2 Corinthians 5:20).

Don't miss the fact that the Spirit of Almighty God makes his appeal through us. That's enablement.

God's redemptive plan is vast and intricate, and each of us is privileged to have a part. You need to pray about your role as a redemptive person. "Remember the chariots!"

5. We are powerless because we are not properly aligned with God's Spirit.

If we are to walk "in step with the Spirit," we must continually decide to be filled or controlled by the Spirit. We must abandon ourselves to his adequacy, submit ourselves to his program, trust him for enablement. We need to depend on and trust in God, acknowledging that we cannot succeed spiritually without his empowering.

How do we get to that place?

First, expect that God deeply desires to use you. Second, maintain the disciplines of a godly life, such as prayer, Bible study, and fellowship with other believers. Third, act on your belief that God desires to use you; put yourself out on a limb!

To keep things in focus, I find it helpful to report for duty each morning. My first waking thoughts confess my need of God. I willingly submit to his agenda for my day, express to him my desire to walk empowered by his Spirit, and thank him ahead of time for his enabling grace. You could do the same thing.

There are millions of sheep out there, lost and wandering without a Shepherd. We're sent to find them. The next chapter will help you to focus upon the "lost flocks" of your network.

Make use of natural relationships.

6

As I turned from 102nd Street onto Glisan, I prayed, "Lord, send some searching nonbelievers across my path."

CASHING IN ON YOUR NETWORKS

Being president of a Bible college has greatly limited my contact with the lost, and I guess my prayer came out of frustration. I long to share Christ with those who haven't those who haven't discovered him.

Heading back toward campus, my mind quickly shifted to other more immediate concerns. Little did I know that God would answer my prayer the very next day.

There was a knock on the door.

"Come on in," I said.

The door opened, and there stood a giant of a man dressed in a wool shirt, faded work jeans, and a pair of heavy-duty suspenders. Well-worn logging boots completed his outfit.

At first I didn't recognize this reincarnation of Paul Bunyan, but when I heard his voice, I knew. He was one of my old high school buddies from the 1950s. I hadn't seen him in almost thirty years.

"Bob, what in the world are you doing here?" I exclaimed.

"Haven't the slightest idea, Joe."

"Well, how did you end up at Multnomah?"

"It was crazy. I was driving down Glisan Street, saw the 'Multnomah School of the Bible' sign, and the next thing I knew I had pulled my truck onto the campus and parked. I jumped out and walked into the closest building."

"You mean this building?"

"Yeah, the one we're in."

"How did you find my office?"

"Well, I asked the girl at the desk about Multnomah. She told me all about your college, and then mentioned that Joe Aldrich was president. I said, 'You mean Joe Aldrich from Vancouver, Washington?' She nodded, pointed down the hall, and said 'His office is right down there.'"

I remembered my prayer. Obviously Bob was the answer! The Lord had sent him my way, and it was my job to get him saved.

"So, what's going on in your life?" I asked with great anticipation.

He explained how his marriage was falling apart and his world was caving in. He was in trouble. I had the answer.

I backed up the evangelical dump truck and pulled the lever. I kept the heat on until he prayed the prayer. I gave him a beautiful new Bible, some quick words of assurance, and sent him on his way with the understanding he'd give me a call and we'd "get together sometime."

I never heard from him again.

Bob wasn't ready, and I wasn't sensitive. I have no question that if I'd listened to him, entered into his pain and met with him as a friend and confidant, he'd have come to a genuine faith in Christ. But that's not what happened. I wanted immediate results; he wanted someone to listen and care.

Where is he today? I don't know.

I pray for Bob, that my stupidity will not hinder him from one day discovering the only answer to his pain and hurt. One thing's for sure: I made his pilgrimage to the Cross more difficult for the next person who attempts to point him in that direction.

Why do I tell that story? First, to remind you that no one bats a thousand when it comes to reaching souls. We all have our failures, even those who have reputations as "successful" soul winners. Second, through a negative example I want to highlight one of the Lord's primary strategies: Concentrate your evangelistic efforts on those who are ready.

The Mission of the Seventy

Let's look once more at the Lord's instructions to the seventy. The boys were sent out with three crucial instructions. They were to *search*, they were to *gain acceptance*, and they were to *stay where they found hospitality*. Their first goal was to discover open channels for the gospel. As we have already noted, the Lord directed them to discover worthy men and worthy homes.

This sensitivity to the readiness and receptivity of both the individual and his social networks is often ignored by contemporary approaches to evangelism. I believe it's fair to say that the typical American church views the community as a collection of isolated strangers, to be confronted with the gospel whenever its members can be interrupted long enough to listen.

On an almost cyclical basis, the concern levels of

church leaders reach the point where they feel compelled to plan and execute another evangelistic "outreach." The community is perceived as a one-dimensional, nameless, faceless mass of businesses, houses, and people with no organic connection. Once the faithful have done enough "evangelism" to salve their collective consciences, they flee to the safety of their facilities, schedules, and programs.

Am I close to the mark?

It's quite possible that you see most evangelism as a violation of social and cultural customs. Perhaps you have concluded that you must abandon all social sensitivities when you speak of Christ. Or it may be that you wonder why God would require you to participate in what seems to be such a psychologically negative experience. Tragically, many have concluded that evangelism must be done in a negative, socially unacceptable manner.

That's not what Jesus had in mind when he gave the seventy their marching orders. Our Lord's instructions to his men provide us with helpful insights into how we can discover webs of relationships which will respond to the gospel.

At the outset, however, I should admit that Jesus did not send out the seventy with instructions that would make them popular and universally received. To the contrary, he told them they would be persecuted and rejected. Birth is never free of pain or difficulty, and evangelism is neither easy nor cheap.

Even with that in mind, it's clear that Jesus had thought deeply about effective ways to reach needy people, ways that neither attacked their dignity nor insulted their customs.

In Matthew 10, Christ sent out the twelve with the command to search for a "worthy" man and a "worthy" home. In Luke's account, the seventy were to look for a "man of peace." Notice that the instructions focused on both the character of the individual and that of his home. They remind us to be sensitive to the condition of the individual and to the social structures in which he lives and functions. Both can provide significant clues about readiness.

The twelve and the seventy were to look for "worthy" men and men of "peace" because the Lord knew these individuals would be most receptive to the gospel. It's likely that such people would already be submissive to the divine institution of government, and they would be practicing basic, biblical principles in their marriage and with their family.

In other words, people who meet these criteria are unlikely to be in rebellion against the laws of the land, and probably will not openly defy the biblical priorities of marriage and family. They have already submitted themselves to substantial areas of biblical revelation. Though unsaved, people who live in obedience to biblical principles will likely be more at "peace" than those who reject biblical norms.

The "man of peace" is likely to be more open than a "man of strife." It is probable that his family will also be inclined to respond. Numerous Scriptures indicate that some are nearer to the Cross than others. Obviously, those who are near are the most receptive to the gospel. While we want to work with people at all stages of readiness, it makes sense to focus on those we believe to be the most ready. Consider these passages:

When Jesus saw that he had answered wisely, he said to him, "You are not far from the kingdom of God" (Mark 12:34).

These people honor me with their lips, but their hearts are far from me (Matthew 15:8).

You who are far away, hear what I have done, you who are near, acknowledge my power! (Isaiah 33:13).

"Peace, peace, to those far and near," says the LORD (Isaiah 57:19).

Scripture reminds us that God causes the rain to fall upon the just and the unjust. Furthermore, the blessings of God accompany obedience to his principles of life. In other words, those who ride in God's car—believers or not—to some extent get God's blessing. Consequently, many nonbelievers are "men of peace." Such people are "near."

The Ethiopian eunuch was "near." Paul wasn't. "Friendship" evangelism wouldn't have worked with the apostle.

As soon as Paul (then Saul) figured out you were a follower of Christ, you were in serious trouble. He was violently opposed to any human witness of Jesus. He threw into prison as many Christians as he could grab.

In contrast, the Ethiopian was reading from Isaiah the prophet and asked Philip to help him understand what he read. His was a "gentle" conversion. Paul's was violent. He either had to hit a wall or God or both. For Paul to convert to Christianity involved a radical cultural and lifestyle change. The very stones that killed Stephen may have been necessary to break up the hard soil of Paul's heart. Certainly, evangelism was costly for Stephen.

It's very possible a geographical or vocational neighbor of yours may be a vile, rebellious, profane individual who could be dangerous to you and your family. Prayer for him may be your only option. He, like Paul, may need an appointment on the Damascus Road.

The mission of the seventy encourages us to search for a point of receptivity. We don't confront the "impersonal community" with a frontal attack and hope someone, somewhere, weakens. The Lord instructs his disciples to search diligently for pre-qualified contacts. Their mission was not primarily to confront people about becoming Christians, but to prepare them for the coming of Christ.

Often our contribution is to discover the people responsive to us and our gifts, establish a redemptive relationship with them, and prepare them for the gifts of another believer who can lead them to Christ. Your contribution may be to find and network those who are open and then bring them under the ministry of those who are gifted in reaping.

"OK, Joe, I think I'm getting the message. Some folks are near, others are far. I'm supposed to find the 'near ones.'"

That's right. Doesn't it make sense to try and "pre-qualify" your audience?

"Yes. But what about those who are led to Christ by a stranger on an airplane? Or what about those who find Christ through a home visit by a stranger? They don't 'pre-qualify' their audiences."

That's true. I can't argue with that. I don't even want to.

"Are you saying that proclaiming Christ to strangers is legitimate?"

Oh my, yes! Absolutely! We must be prepared to give the gospel to those we don't know. Some, however, are particularly gifted for those circumstances. Most are not. "Cold contacts" aren't the only circumstances that require readiness.

"What do you mean by that?"

The gospel flows down webs of relationships. Perhaps 90 percent of believers are not gifted in "door to door" evangelism. Most are not reapers.

"I understand that, but what do you mean by this 'webs of relationship' stuff? What are you talking about?"

Each of us has an *oikos*.

"Oh, great. Should we see a doctor? C'mon, Joe, make yourself plain! What do you mean by an 'oinkus'"?

An *oikos*. I thought you'd never ask! An *oikos* is a circle of influence or a network made up of people related to one another through birth, career, or common interests.

"You mean, sort of a social system?"

Exactly. A social system made up of those who are in regular contact with each other through common ties and activities.

"Like neighbors, families, relatives, and associates at work?"

You got it!

The *Oikos* Perspective

Although evangelism is personal in response, it is not individual in focus. Every individual must make a personal decision, but no individual should be viewed in isolation. In other words, I don't go out to "pick off" individuals. I claim entire networks. I visualize the gospel flowing down webs of relationships, reaching individual after individual who know and are somehow related to each other. This requires an " *oikos* perspective."

Oikos is a Greek word for "household." The first Christians referred to themselves as the "household of God." The house was both a fellowship or community as well as a place of meeting. Paul's familiar dialogue with the Philippian jailer illustrates his *oikos* perspective.

About midnight Paul and Silas were praying and singing hymns to God, and the other prisoners were listening to them. Suddenly there was such a violent earthquake that the foundations of the prison were shaken. At once all the prison doors flew open, and everybody's chains came loose. The jailer woke up, and when he saw the prison doors open, he drew his sword and was about to kill himself because he thought the prisoners had escaped. But Paul shouted, "Don't harm yourself! We are all here!"

The jailer called for lights, rushed in and fell trembling before Paul and Silas. He then brought them out and asked, "Sirs, what must I do to be saved?"

They replied, "Believe in the Lord Jesus, and you will be saved—you and your household" (Acts 16:25-31).

Paul visualized more than the personal response of the jailer. He anticipated the flow of the gospel into the jailer's *oikos*.

He also may have anticipated it flowing into a second *oikos*, one that's not usually noticed in this passage. Did you observe that none of the prisoners left their cells when the prison doors flew open? "About midnight Paul and Silas were praying and singing hymns to God, *and the other prisoners were listening to them*," says verse 25. Then came the earthquake, and open flew the doors. But nobody left: "Don't harm yourself! *We are all here!*" shouted Paul.

Could it be that the prisoners were too interested in what Paul was saying to bother about escaping? Could it be that the prisoners formed a second *oikos*, a community of men living in the same culture and under the same circumstances, who wanted to hear about what made two of their fellow prisoners so happy? Luke doesn't mention if any of them were saved, but I'd bet we'll meet a few of them when we get to heaven. Paul had a habit of leaving a trail of Christians wherever he went.

Many Christians do. A practice which typifies most of them is described in the passages that follow.

> At Caesarea there was a man named Cornelius, a centurion in what was known as the Italian Regiment. He and all his family were devout and God-fearing; he gave generously to those in need and prayed to God regularly.
>
> The following day he [Peter] arrived in Caesarea. Cornelius was expecting them and had called together his relatives and close friends. [His oikos]
>
> Talking with him, Peter went inside and found a large gathering of people [the oikos of Cornelius] (Acts 10:1- 2, 24, 27).

Following Cornelius's conversion, Peter reflects on this experience as he explains why he, a Jew, ministered to this Gentile and his family. He quotes the words of Cornelius:

> He [Cornelius] told us how he had seen an angel appear in his house and say, "Send to Joppa for Simon who is called Peter. He will bring you a message through which you and all your household will be saved" (Acts 11:13- 14).

The Lord opened Lydia's heart and she responded to Paul's message. Luke writes:

> When she and the members of her household were bap- tized, she invited us to her home (Acts 16:15).

While in Corinth, Luke records that Paul:

. . . left the synagogue and went next door to the house of Titius Justus, a worshiper of God. Crispus, the synagogue ruler, and his entire household believed in the Lord (Acts 18:7-8).

Paul himself wrote that,

Yes, I also baptized the household of Stephanas . . . (1 Corinthians 1:16).

Jesus said to Zacchaeus:

Today salvation has come to this house (Luke 19:9).

When Christ healed the official's son, John records:

So he and all his household believed (John 4:53).

Is it any wonder that when the Lord sent the seventy, he gave them specific instructions to look for worthy homes? We shouldn't be surprised that once they located such a home and were received into it, they were commanded to

Stay in that house . . . Do not move around from house to house (Luke 10:7).

To the twelve he said:

Whatever town or village you enter, search for some worthy person there and stay at his house until you leave (Matthew 10:11).

An *oikos* is a social system built around family and friends. The majority of friends usually come from what is known as a free associational group. Such groups could include:

1. Fraternal clubs
2. Service organizations

3. Churches
4. Athletic groups
5. Political action groups
6. Hobby-centered groups
7. Business and professional associations
8. Recreational/sporting groups
9. Health clubs
10. Symphony guilds
11. Unions
12. Supper clubs, gourmet groups
13. Volunteer activities
14. Baby-sitting co-ops

All these groups provide windows to the community. Through access doors like these you can build relationships with non-Christians. Networking with people around a common interest or cause is a natural and powerful way to position yourself for redemptive results.

Implications of the *Oikos* Perspective

This biblical emphasis on the *oikos* as a center for evangelism implies several things. Let's look at some of them.

1. For most of us, effective evangelism begins with networking.

Not all evangelism depends upon influencing social systems. A small percentage among us are especially gifted reapers. These important members of the redemptive team aren't as dependent upon penetrating social systems and cultivating hard-packed soil as are the rest of us. They do depend, however, upon those with cultivating gifts. There is no reaping without cultivating and sowing. That's a reminder that we are laborers *together* with God.

Soulcrafters don't solo. Sometimes a neighborhood network is a good place to start.

I was speaking in Colorado on "Cultivating, Sowing, and Reaping: The Three Phases of Evangelism." After the service, a young woman approached and asked, "Joe, do you remember me?"

I didn't. I told the truth.

"Well, I used to baby-sit for your son."

Oh, that's right. But that was ten years ago! How would she expect me to remember?

"I want you to know that two years ago someone shared Christ with me, and I became a believer. But the reason I trusted Christ was because of what I saw ten or fifteen years ago."

"What you saw ten years ago?"

"Yes! When I used to walk across the green strip of grass between your house and mine, it was like going from darkness to light. I couldn't figure out what made your home and family so different from mine."

"You're kidding!" I said.

"No, I'm serious. After I put your kids to bed, I used to go into the den and pull books off the shelf to try to find out what made you tick. When I'd leave your house to return home, it was like going from light back to darkness again."

Then she asked a very perceptive question.

"Is that why you used to wax my dad's car?"

Her dad loved automobiles, but couldn't do much to maintain them because of a heart condition. I'd learned that if you love what somebody else loves, you'll be loved. That's just what happened.

I'd ask her father to give me his car keys, then I'd wash and wax his auto. He'd pull up a folding chair and we'd talk and talk. Not about spiritual things. He wasn't ready. His family was part of our neighborhood network, and we did lots of things together.

I'm delighted to report that the gospel has gone down through webs of relationships into that family unit. It started with a can of wax, a listening ear, and a curious baby-sitter. My prayer is that the entire *oikos* will be saved.

2. A networking strategy will influence your approach to evangelism.

Reaching an *oikos* takes time. It takes preparation. Usually you have to plan ahead.

Football season doesn't come until fall. If your son plays the game, you may have to wait until the season starts to get to know all the family units associated with that network. And that's just the beginning. It takes time to position yourself in such a social system. It may take years of faithful prayer and service before a redemptive people-flow begins in your vocational network. But it's unlikely to happen at all if you don't make it your goal.

Two of my pre-Christian friends are avid duck hunters. The Portland area's regional director for the Fellowship of Christian Athletes also hunts. My goal is to get them all together around something we share in common, and let God work through our association. It's a natural "hookup." The fact that my FCA friend was also an All-Pro football player adds another dimension.

3. To influence networks, you must reach individuals.

My wife and I are praying that God will allow us to see six people from our networks trust Christ this year. Having identified those whom we believe to be the most responsive, we anticipate that the Lord, our co-laborer, will work with, in, and through us to bring insight, conviction, and new birth to our as-yet-unsaved friends.

Receptivity Factors

Let's suppose you are starting from scratch. To this point you really haven't thought of penetrating and influencing webs of relationships. Perhaps you don't know where to begin, or how to determine receptivity. What follows are some broad clues which may help to narrow your focus and increase your effectiveness.

1. The mobility factor.

Communities are either growing, stable, or declining. Generally speaking, the first group is easier to reach than the other two.

Stable populations tend to support the status quo and resist change. Declining communities may become defensive and hard to reach when people start to leave.

Growing communities, on the other hand, attract newcomers who have been uprooted both geographically and socially. Consequently, these folks are open to establishing new social and vocational networks.

Ruthe and I found that as we moved from one new neighborhood to another, we had many opportunities to build friendships. There are fences to be built, lawns to be planted, sprinkler systems to install. All these activities provide great opportunities to pitch in, pound a nail, and cement a friendship. The nature of your community should influence your methodology and strategy.

2. The residence factor.

Permanent or temporary housing situations also influence receptivity. Ruthe and I managed apartments for seven years, and we discovered that transients are a challenge to reach. People who visualize their housing as temporary are less likely to be open to building long-term relationships. But they can be reached! Those who rent apartments and condominiums are often single, divorced, or part of a single-parent family. Their unique needs provide good opportunities for perceptive Christians.

On the other hand, the stable, well-established neighborhood can be very resistant to the gospel. It may take years for you to influence your neighbors toward the Cross. Even if you have lived there for a long time, neighbors may become suspicious about "new ideas" coming into the block. Don't let that stop you from letting your light shine! If you're faithful about representing Christ in your neighborhood, God may have some surprises up his sleeve. Be ready to take advantage of them when he makes his move!

3. The ethnic factor.

Cross-cultural evangelists confront the barriers of language, culture, and values. The twelve apostles were told to avoid the Gentiles and the Samaritans, and to focus upon reaching their own people. Peter had a great struggle "rewiring" himself to minister to the household of Cornelius, the Gentile. Paul spent most of his ministry focusing on the Gentile world.

Those of races different from your own are reachable, but to do so involves great sensitivity. Paul became a Jew to win the Jews, a Gentile to win the Gentiles, and weak to win the weak. He became a naturalized citizen of their world and adjusted his methodology to their culture.

4. The economic factor.

Income levels segment populations into certain class structures. The blue-collar worker lives in an entirely different world than the upper-class, business executive. His values and experiences are different. His recreation, use of leisure time, and his associations are usually different. The two groups often share little in common and don't have much to talk about.

Even so, remember that the gospel somehow got into the household of Caesar himself (Philippians 4:22). That may mean that, somewhere along the way, a poor Christian led a wealthy pagan to the Lord. If you find yourself in a situation where you're surrounded by those of unlike economic status, don't give up hope. Recognize that your road will no doubt be rougher than most, but it's not impossible. It also means you'll have to get serious about prayer—a not entirely lamentable situation.

5. The religious factor.

Generally, those who come out of a religious background like yours are easier for you to reach. You normally have some shared presuppositions, some points of commonality. In some religions, faith and culture are one and the same. Consequently, people who become Christians face tremendous cultural changes. Those caught up in cults are often a challenge to reach for this very reason.

Look for those with religious upbringings similar to yours. You'll have a head start in your effort to bring them to Christ.

6. The experience factor.

Life experience is often a key to your reception by others. An "experience inventory" can be an encouraging exercise. We do learn from experience, and what we learn, we can share.

To witness is more than describing the person and work of Christ, important as that is. To witness is to tell of your experience of Christ and how he has enabled you to overcome the liabilities, problems, and crises of life. People respond to someone who has "been there" and found a way out. People respond to those who are authentic, approachable, and willing to speak of their own failures and successes.

The Discovery Principle

Sometimes it's fun to leave the best to last. So you've discovered a worthy man or woman. They've welcomed you into their lives. Why should you "stay in that house" and not "move around from house to house"? Because, friend, you have discovered your *oikos*. You have uncovered those who will be spiritually responsive.

Here's the principle: *No one will receive Christ through you who will not receive you first.*

You are the message. Those who respond to you socially will be open to you spiritually. Notice our Lord's instructions to the seventy:

> *He who listens to you listens to me; he who rejects you rejects me* . . . (Luke 10:16).

If folks reject you, they're going to reject you as a messenger of Christ. Their reception of Christ often depends upon their reception of you. The Semitic law of the messenger said that "the emissary of the man is as the man himself." In other words, the "worthy man's" hospitality to the disciples implies his reception of Christ.

Where do you go from here? I'll suggest just two things.

First, identify your networks. To what groups, clubs, or associations do you belong? Who would be most receptive within these networks? Think of contacts within that *oikos* which would qualify as "worthy men and women." Jot them down.

Second, begin to pray that God will use you in your present networks and that he will help you to build new ones.

"Charity begins at home," an old saying goes. I'm not sure I like the idea, but it might grow on me if you changed the first word to "Evangelism." *Evangelism* begins at home . . . especially in your "home neighborhood." Which *oikos* in yours looks ready?

Pray earnestly for specific individuals.

7

Sonya risks everything to communicate Christ. Should her Communist countrymen discover her faithful ministry, she

CULTIVATING YOUR CUL-DE-SAC

would be incarcerated for at least ten years. But the threat of imprisonment has not intimidated this modern-day heroine.

Surrounded by the ever-present wolf pack, her evangelistic options are extremely limited. She dare not speak openly of Christ. She has no books, tapes, or films to loan out. Her life is her only weapon. Like Christ, her "life is the light."

Sonya is a twentieth-century example of the ancient prophet Isaiah's reminder that our light rises as the morning sun when we stoop to serve. Our righteousness goes before us when we clothe the naked, and the glory of God becomes our rear guard when the soup's on and the door's open. People come to Christ because of Sonya's ministry.

Why is Sonya so effective in evangelism despite the adverse conditions she faces? Here is what she says:

I'm not sure I know all the reasons why, but let me give you an example. I was going through the check stand in the village grocery store. As I glanced out the window, a mother and her two children caught my eye. Their poverty was obvious. Thin, bony hands, sunken eyes, and tattered clothes underscored their acute need. They clung together outside the store. All they could think about was a decent meal and some warm clothes. My heart was strangely tugged toward them.

I picked up my two sacks of groceries, walked out the door, and handed this dear mother and her kids my groceries. Their faces lit up. We made small talk and I left.

The Lord prompted me to pray for these dear folks, so I did. Several weeks later I spotted them again. I followed them home. Now I knew where they lived. I continued in prayer.

The Lord prompted me to buy some women's shoes and take them to her. I didn't know her size, but figured the Lord did. I purchased the shoes, hiked over to her house, delivered them, and made small talk. I couldn't mention Christ, but I continued in prayer.

The Lord prompted me to buy the children some sweaters. I made the purchase and made my way over to deliver them. The kids were delighted. I visited with them for a bit, then headed home. I continued in prayer.

The Lord prompted me to take over a couple of hankies. No big deal, but apparently it was part of God's agenda. We visited again, and then I returned home. I continued in prayer.

Then the Lord prompted me to do something for

which I had to pray a little longer. He apparently
wanted me to bring over some women's underwear
. . . a somewhat unusual request. I prayed about it
a little longer before I was convinced. The purchase
made, I showed up on her doorstep and delivered
my package. The dear lady looked inside and was
elated, then became very upset.

"How is it," she asked, "that you are able to listen
in on the conversations between my husband and
myself?"

"I don't know what you're talking about," was my
reply.

"Then how do you know what our needs are?" she
asked.

"God tells me."

"He must! Several months ago I was waiting for the
bus. The street was muddy. I stepped into the bus
as it was pulling away and left a shoe in the mud.
It was the only pair I owned. When I got home, I
explained to my husband what had happened. As
you know, Sonya, he's an alcoholic. He drinks up
everything he brings home. He told me if I was
dumb enough to leave a shoe in the mud, I could
go without shoes. That afternoon you showed up
with the shoes.

"Several weeks later the weather started getting
cold. School was soon to start. I asked my husband
if I could get some sweaters for the kids to replace
their rags. I got cursed out for even suggesting it;
then you showed up with the sweaters.

"The kids caught cold, and I asked if I could get
them some hankies. It was just a little thing. The
answer was a clear and decisive NO. Yes, you know.

You showed up with the hankies.

"As you know, I've been looking for work. I finally found a prospective employer who thought he might have a place for me. He told me I'd have to have a physical. I knew I'd feel a lot more secure about the physical if I had some decent underwear. [You can appreciate her concern. Didn't your mom always tell you not to wear the underwear with a tear in it? You might get in an accident and end up on a stretcher with holes in your underwear, and the doctor would think your mother was terrible.]

"I explained to my husband about the job possibility and pled with him to allow me to buy some underwear. He ridiculed me and denied my request. And you showed up with the underwear."

Is it any wonder that this dear mother came to faith in Christ? Is it hard to see why she came to believe that God was real and cared about her and her needs? How can you argue with someone who gives and gives and gives? How can you argue with someone who trusts God's agenda, and as a co-laborer with him, moves out expecting him to give the increase?

A Review with Two

We haven't checked in with Amos and Zechariah for quite a while now. I wonder what they've learned? Let's check in and see.

"Well, Zach, we've been here for several days. How do you think things are going?"

"I miss my own bed, Amos. I know that, for sure! There's no place like home, you know."

"It's not exactly the Hilton, I grant you. But I'm

beginning to see the Lord's wisdom in all this."

"How's that?"

"Remember the Master's instructions about finding a worthy home and a man of peace?"

"Yeah, and staying in that home."

"And having to leave all our cash behind. Zach, I'm starting to understand the Lord's strategy: Camp close to a worthy man!"

"And a worthy family. Don't forget the family! Have you noticed how many people know Mary and Isaiah? They've got tons of friends."

"What the Lord said makes sense. Who wouldn't be attracted to a worthy man, a man of peace? He really sets the tone for the whole family."

"And their hospitality sort of opens up their whole web of friends to us."

"Yeah, and have you noticed that most of their friends seem open and friendly? I really believe that when the Lord comes to town, we'll have a crowd of folks out to hear him."

"Most of them are friends of Mary and Isaiah. This really gets me excited, Amos! The gospel of the kingdom's going to flow right down those webs of relationships."

"Right, and the fact that Mary and Isaiah have been so hospitable to us sort of automatically bonds us to their friends. You know, if Isaiah accepts us, his friends probably will, too."

"And they'll be open to our message. I think they're going to love Christ when he comes."

"So who needs the Hilton?"

How Do You Cultivate a Soul?

Cultivation is an appeal to the heart through the building of a relationship. Let's learn some things about cultivation from Sonya's illustration.

1. Sonya responded to a need.

Beginning with a need is a good strategy. Most of our acquaintances in this country don't suffer from malnourishment of the body. Many souls, however, are impoverished. They lack a sense of security and significance, despite all their worldly marks of achievement and success.

Let's be open to need! Ministry often begins at a point of need. Lots of folks just need a friend.

2. Sonya responded without any assurance of the outcome.

Faith comes in when you're uncertain how things will turn out. Once you have thrown a redemptive switch, you see people in a different light. Every contact has redemptive potential. Each interaction has impact. We view all involvements as divinely significant, *whether we ever see the results.*

If you're thinking evangelism, if you're burdened for the lost, if you're gifted to meet specific needs, it's a natural thing to hand out groceries with no guarantees . . . except that you're a laborer together with God.

3. Sonya responded with no awareness of the details of God's partnership.

Sonya brought shoes, not knowing that a shoe had been lost and a replacement denied by an abusive, alcoholic husband. She brought sweaters, not knowing that new sweaters had been eliminated. She brought hankies, not knowing they had been disallowed. She brought underwear, not knowing of the doctor's appointment or of the husband's cruel and self-centered behavior.

Sonya did it all, not realizing the incredible sequence or timing of events. Note well, my friend, that God took the simple gifts of Sonya and turned each one into a miracle . . . without Sonya's knowledge. That's the kind of God with whom we co- labor.

4. Sonya took the initiative.

Sonya saw a need and met it. She did it in the name of Christ, even though she dared not mention him. She took the initiative despite the risk. Sonya refused to flee to a self- absorbed harbor of safety. The initial cost of her action was a couple of sacks of groceries—not, by the way, an insignificant cost in Soviet Russia. But if she hadn't spent the money, the ultimate cost might have been horrible beyond words.

5. Sonya understood soulcraft.

Repeated demonstrations of love build spiritual lever-age. Sonya's friend was beginning to fall in love with Christ; she just didn't know it yet. All the love, all the care and attention she received was simply Christ reach-ing out through a submissive, obedient servant. Shoes, sweaters, hankies, and underwear given in the name of Christ built momentum. These were wonderful gifts!

Sonya's greatest gift, however, was herself. Moms love kids. Moms want kids to be adequately fed and clothed. "Love my kid, meet my kid's need, and you're a friend. Love what I love, and you're loved. Listen to me, share my pain, bear my burden, encourage my heart, and you're my friend. Let me help you, and you're also my friend."

If they'll receive you, they're likely to receive your friend, who "sticks closer than a brother."

6. Sonya was a woman of prayer.

Prayer changes things. Not all those folks in your *oikos* are going to be receptive. Prayer can change that. You'll face opposition—prayer can equip you to handle rejection. Prayer revamps your expectations, it opens you to God's agenda.

Note that Sonya was open to the prompting of the Lord. Note that each prompting was part of a larger scenario. She brought shoes with no awareness that shoes had just been the center of a firestorm. Unknown to her, the next big blowup centered around sweaters. God had her bring sweaters.

Prayer must not simply focus on the spiritual predicament of the lost; it must also encompass their physical needs. Prayer predisposes us to sense the prompting of the Spirit.

7. Sonya had a sense of timing.

"Sonya, how are you able to listen in on the arguments between my husband and myself? How do you know what our needs are?" the woman asked. "God tells me," Sonya replied.

Sonya's friend was no fool. She observed the uncanny way in which Sonya appeared each time with exactly the right answer to her needs. Furthermore, she sensed the genuineness of Sonya's friendship. And what did that lead to? She was prepared for Sonya's answer. She didn't reject it. It made sense to her that only God could work out the details, that only God could enable someone to be so loving, that only God could move someone to become a servant to another's needs. She heard the music and was ready for the words.

8. Sonya had patience.

Patience is a missing ingredient in most approaches to evangelism. We want visible, tangible, recordable results NOW. We jump from method to method, guru to guru, and are uniformly disappointed. We "try something" for a few weeks or months, and then jump ship.

The problem is we've confused evangelism with methodology. We've missed the reality of evangelism as a fundamental way of living which utilizes methods appropriate to individual gifts and abilities. We are event-centered rather than process-centered. We are unwilling to do the hard labor of "cultivating." If we don't "reap in a week" we quit, despite the fact that no cultivating or sowing has transpired. We flit from blossom to blossom, instead of "staying in that house."

In many cases, cultivating takes years. Bob Griffin, one of my heroes, has been a pilot for Wycliffe (JAARS) for years. While serving in Ecuador, he befriended a military commander who made it clear their friendship depended upon Bob keeping mum about Christ. The commander asked Bob if he would fly supplies to some military bases in the jungle—the army was losing too many supplies from overturned canoes and slippery jungle trails. Bob said yes.

Remote airstrips were built, and for several years Bob ferried in supplies by plane. One day his friend announced he was being reassigned and would be leaving the area. He requested that Bob fly him to his new assignment, even though he could have taken any military plane he desired. While in the air, he turned to Bob, gripped his arm, and said, "This is probably the last time I'll see you. Your life is so different—I want what you have."

Several years of silent witness and service earned Bob a twenty-minute window of time during which the commander received Christ.

Lifestyle evangelism may take time. Often it doesn't. The question is, are you willing to wait however long it takes?

9. *Sonya journeyed out of her world and into theirs.*

Sonya didn't wait for needy people to come to her. She went into a stranger's home and accepted her hospitality, even though the marks of poverty and alcoholism were obvious.

This lady treasured Sonya's friendship. The barriers of poverty and an alcoholic husband did not keep Sonya from reaching out and being a friend. Love can do that.

10. *Sonya nurtured a powerful bond.*

There's nothing like two strangers sharing life together over a period of time. The social bonding that takes place becomes a significant factor in effective evangelism. It predisposes the person to openness.

As we have said, no one is likely to receive Christ through you who will not receive you first. We all need friends. Sonya's whole ministry was built upon the deep-seated human need to love and be loved. A caring bond allows for natural communication of the gospel and provides a healthy context for follow-up once conversion takes place. It is normal for the new convert to attend church where his/her friend belongs.

Cultivating in Your Cul-de-sac

Amos and Zach went to work in their *oikos*. Isaiah and Mary welcomed them into their home and were intrigued by what they saw and heard. The word got out. The telephone lines were humming with chatter and speculation. The soft glow of olive oil lamps provided light for spirited discussions around the evening meal. Time seemed to stop. Escaping to the Hilton was forgotten long ago. The *oikos* of Isaiah and Mary became the focus of ministry.

Fine for Amos and Zach! But how do you begin to

mark the networks in your own life?

1. Do an inventory of your networks.

List relatives, friends, and associates with whom you have regular contact. Record names of aunts, uncles, spouses, nieces, nephews, and other extended family members. Make note of those friends and neighbors with whom you are in regular communication. Pencil in the names of associates at work, at the club, or folks with whom you rub shoulders in civic and social activities. It's important to have a visual record of your most "reach-able" friends.

2. Network your present acquaintances.

As you look through the list of your *oikos*, link those who know each other. Note, for example, those at the office who enjoy a common friendship with you. Link those in the industry who know each other. Network relatives, professional associates, neighbors, and friends. It is important to begin to visualize "households" which are candidates for your influence.

3. Identify potential networks.

Perhaps your *oikos* potential seems limited. To this point you haven't really flowed into the homes, lives, and experiences of many non-Christians. Listen, there's no time like now to get started!

How about a garden club, a Pop Warner football league, a neighborhood association, the PTA, a trade association, a service club, or the parents of your children's friends? How about monitoring the maternity ward at your local hospital and volunteering to bring over meals for the first week when mom and her new baby come home? The Mormons are doing it in almost every hospital in the country. It's the old story—aim at nothing, and you'll hit it every time.

4. Target receptive individuals.

Scan your list of names and identify those who seem most responsive to you. You're looking for "worthy" men or women, people of peace within your networks. I don't mean you should ignore the troubled, the unruly, or the vile, but it makes sense to start your evangelistic efforts with those who appear most receptive. The following are some factors that influence personal receptivity:

a. The circumstances under which your friend learned about Christianity.

b. The caricatures which have distorted your friend's grasp of the gospel.

c. The Christians your friend has known and their influence upon him or her.

d. The previous attempts (if any) to evangelize the friend.

e. The individual's family loyalties and the role religion plays in determining them.

f. The individual's degree of satisfaction/dissatisfaction with life.

g. The nature and stability of his or her interpersonal relationships.

h. Where your friend sits on a continuum between strong opposition and acceptance of the gospel.

i. The condition of the soil of his or her soul (Matthew 13).

j. The nature and frequency of contacts with the church.

k. The transitions facing the individual, whether social, emotional, physical, financial, geographical, etc.

Not only is it important to be aware of factors which shape receptivity, we must be alert to signs of readiness. I once received a phone call from a college student at a California university who explained that she and her Christian sisters were studying my book *Life-style Evangelism*. As they reviewed the section on "Determining Readiness," she realized that her friend down the hall met the requirements for readiness.

As soon as the study was over, she grabbed her Bible, headed down the hall to her friend's room, presented the gospel, and called me to say that she had a brand new sister in Christ. That woman was ready! People show they're ready when:

- they enjoy being with their Christian friends.
- their religious background and experience ceases to be a hindrance.
- they have responded positively to the "seed planting" efforts of their Christian friend.
- they become aware that the gospel may contain solutions to their felt needs.
- they are curious about religious things.
- they are willing to speak of their own spiritual pilgrimage.
- they take the initiative to include you in their social activities.
- they are willing to participate in some harvest events.

The earliest and most significant evidence of receptivity is simply their willingness to be your friend, that they accept you into their web of relationships. In the early stages of a relationship, it will not be possible to observe all the evidences of receptivity. As the relationship grows, you will begin to see confirming responses along the lines described.

A familiar axiom among salesmen states, "I will not begin talking about my solution until I'm certain my prospect is eager to hear about it." Try to identify those who have the potential for becoming eager to hear about the gospel. Their receptivity toward you as a person is a big clue. If they like what they see of Christ in you (even though they don't know it's Christ), they will respond to your explanation of the vibrant hope of a Christ-filled life.

5. Respond to individual differences.

Evangelism should be tailor-made. Because of the great diversity of ways in which people travel to Calvary, it's important to recognize, respect, and act upon individual differences. That's why it's imperative that we get to know people.

Our actions are controlled by our attitudes, and our attitudes are generally shaped by our experiences. If one of our friends has had several bad experiences with well-meaning evangelists, it's likely he has a bad attitude toward any kind of of evangelism. It is unlikely he will act to receive Christ until those negative attitudes are changed.

Often it is the loving, sensitive care of a Christian friend that re-programs his "experience bank" with positive examples, thus changing his attitude toward Christianity. It is important, therefore, to know something of your non-Christian friend's background and experience.

6. Become naturalized citizens of their world.

A major key to effective evangelism is to find that

point in an individual's life where the gospel becomes good news, then tailor your presentation to that point. That's why witnessing to a stranger is such a difficult challenge.

Evangelism is most productive when we recognize and respond to the uniqueness of the individual. Evangelism can be remembering birthdays and anniversaries, celebrating their successes, enjoying their hospitality, participating in their areas of interest and enjoyment.

Evangelism also involves feeling around the rim of their souls for cracks, and using this information as a starting point for introducing the gospel.

If a marriage is falling apart, part of the Good News is that God heals marriages. If sickness strikes, part of the Good News is that God can give grace sufficient to face even the shadow of death. If guilt cripples and distorts, part of the Good News is that in Christ there is forgiveness. If lack of security and significance haunts a tortured soul, the Good News is that we can become eternally significant sons and daughters of the King. If material success doesn't satisfy, the gospel brings water that quenches eternal thirst. If the fear of death has crippled life, the gospel proclaims that Jesus conquered death. If the prospect of judgment torments the soul, the gospel offers the only relief. If someone is crippled by destructive habits and sinful patterns, only the gospel can bring deliverance and freedom.

I suggest that you develop a spiritual inventory of those people who seem to be responding to you. It wouldn't hurt to write down information concerning their religious background and experience, their family situation, their hobbies, interests, and achievements. Note everything you can think of that might be important to that person.

7. Develop a gift-driven plan.

Let's face it, the effectiveness of what you do is going to be closely linked with the creative use of your gifts. Notice I said "*your* gifts." Not somebody else's. If you don't have five loaves and fishes in your sack, you can't feed folks fish and chips. Proverbs 24:3-4 states that "Any enterprise is built by wise planning, becomes strong through common sense, and profits wonderfully by keeping abreast of the facts."

8. Begin with an inventory of your gifts.

Whatever you can do with a degree of skill, whether it be listening or pounding nails, is a gift. So are those things which bring you satisfaction and joy. You may not be an expert golfer, but do you enjoy playing? Perhaps you could learn from your neighbor! Maybe you get great pleasure out of entertaining, or perhaps fishing is your thing.

God uses screwdrivers, hammers, bran muffins, and coffee. A screwdriver driven by a loving heart is a potent tool for evangelism. It might be helpful to take a paper and pencil and actually jot down your own gifts, abilities, hobbies, and interests.

9. Offer your gifts to God as instruments for noble purposes.

A specific act of presenting your gifts to the Lord is an important step in becoming a redemptive person. It will help to remember that your gifts are not simply for your own satisfaction and pleasure. They are God's tools to be used for his purposes. They are the instruments he will use to thrust you into a place of significant ministry. He won't use what you don't have, nor will he expect you to do what you're not gifted to do.

10. Use your gifts as a clue to the shape of your ministry.

If you drive a pickup to work instead of a sedan, you may be on to the kind of ministry God has chosen for you—especially if you have a gun rack in the truck's back window. If you're more comfortable with a hammer than a calculator or prefer a chainsaw to a computer, your ministry will reflect your preferences. God may use you to network a bunch of four-wheelers or even eighteen-wheelers.

If you love to cook, cook for the glory of God. If you enjoy entertaining, entertain for the glory of God. If you are skilled at listening, listen for the glory of God. If you can fix a toilet, do it for the glory of God. If you can play tennis, do it for the glory of God.

For the glory of God? Right! Engage yourself in using your skills and abilities to serve others at their point of need. God is glorified every time his light and life break through darkness. Serve to "win as many as possible." Do it with a serving, giving spirit in the name of Christ.

Do it in the name of Christ? Yes, do it with the awareness that your service is ultimately for him. Do it with the awareness that you go under his authority, empowered by his indwelling presence.

11. Don't undersell your gifts.

Your abilities will reveal whether you are a doer or a talker, a cultivator or a reaper. They will help you determine whether you are a visible, upfront-type persuader, or a behind-the-scenes persuader. They'll clue you in on whether you are more comfortable in public or in private. It may be you're most powerful under the sink, fixing the garbage disposal for a friend.

Don't minimize the power of any such deeds. Don't sell yourself short if "all" you can do is fix a broken pipe, weld a cracked block, wire a fixture, tend a child, or clean a house. Done in the name of Christ and for his glory, such actions become Spirit-powered weapons which are mighty through God to the pulling down of strongholds.

12. Blend your gifts with others for maximum impact.

If you want to get to know your neighbors, but feel a little weak on the hospitality side of things, invite over a Christian couple who have the gift of hospitality. Alert them that your neighbors are not yet followers of Christ, and let their gifts knit you to your neighbor. They can set the tone, help your neighbors feel at ease, and help bond you to them. If you're alert, you may learn some secrets of hospitality by observing what your friends say and do.

If your neighbor is an avid fisherman and you're not, find out if a fellow church member is an angling fanatic. Get the two worm draggers together, and you go along for the ride. Their common love of fishing may forge a friendship with redemptive consequences.

Perhaps God is giving you the opportunity to prepare some folks in your *oikos* for the coming of an evangelist. Again, you are blending gifts. You are doing your part by cultivating and sowing. The evangelist will exercise his gift of reaping and perhaps be the vehicle through which some of your friends come to Christ.

If it should be your privilege to have a quality evangelist in your area:

- Evaluate which friends would be most likely to attend a crusade.

- Make a definite commitment to God that you will invite them.

- Determine when and how you will invite them to the crusade.

- Enlist a core of believers to pray with you for the specific men and women you plan to invite.

- Invite them!

I often follow in the wake of my wife, Ruthe. She is the one who networks most easily. Her interpersonal skills far exceed mine. She is surrounded by friends who think she's the fourth member of the trinity.

Most of all, she is a genuine friend who just loves people in very specific, tangible ways. And they find Christ!

13. Don't watch the clock.

It may take time, perhaps years, to see a friend find Christ. Don't give up! Bathe the relationship in prayer. Pray for boldness and open doors. Have faith that God will use the witness of your serving lifestyle. Pray that you may have the privilege of reaping or that you can prepare the individual for the reaping skills of another.

Can you do this? I know you can! Believe me, getting people to the foot of the Cross is an exciting, challenging, fulfilling opportunity. It's not always easy, but God never leaves you alone to fend for yourself. *You can help people find Christ through your creative efforts.*

Isn't that what it's all about?

Avoid pitfalls which hamper evangelism.

8

GROWING CROPS, NOT WEEDS

Truck drivers are a breed apart. I learned that the hard way.

While laboring over a seminary Hebrew assignment, I became convicted that an "eighteen-wheeler" who lived down a few doors from me needed to be evangelized . . . right now, whether he felt like it or not. I set aside my Hebrew text and waltzed down the sidewalk to his apartment. I could hear the TV blaring as I knocked on his door. It swung open just as the bedroom door closed—his live-in girlfriend was there.

I didn't beat around the bush. I asked him to shut off the TV and proceeded to evangelize him. I dumped the whole spiel. Buried the poor soul.

Contrary to my naive expectations, he wasn't interested in the Bible, Christianity, or Christ. He told me so point-blank.

Is it possible that the Lord will use my feeble attempt at evangelizing the trucker? Perhaps. While my approach was probably not the ideal, God's Word does not return void. So should I continue to proceed with such hasty methods? Probably not.

I overlooked some options. He and I lived in the same apartment building. We could have become friends. I could have taken an interest in his world and been more sensitive to his state of readiness. Ruthe and I could have had him over for dinner. Bachelors love home-cooked meals. We could have networked him with other believers in the apartment complex.

As I reflect over that experience, I realize that I missed the opportunity to spend a day traveling with him in the truck. I'd have loved it. It could have made a big difference. So where did I fail?

Evangelistic Pitfalls to Avoid

1. I moved too quickly to a reaping mode.

This trucker wasn't a stranger I'd never see again. He was a tenant in the building Ruthe and I managed. We saw him on a regular basis. That's a different set of circumstances than what you'd encounter in witnessing to a stranger on an airplane.

If your goal is to influence an entire apartment complex, a business office, or some similar group, it is not wise to be premature. Why not? "The word" will spread and soon you'll be out of business: "Look out for Aldrich, he's after your soul."

Readiness is crucial in "thinking networks." It's easy to unplug a potential network by moving too quickly.

2. I assumed that what worked at the university would work in the apartment complex.

Ruthe and I had the joy of seeing many students find Christ when we were on Campus Crusade staff at the University of Oregon. The methods we used were appropriate to the college scene of the 1960s. (They are less appropriate now, by the way, because today's collegiate scene has vastly changed.)

College freshmen and truck drivers have little in common. A typical eighteen-year-old freshman away from home for the first time is lonely, searching, and open. While there may not be a typical trucker, one with a gal at every stop is hardened, suspicious, and often hostile. A quick trip through the Four Laws with an unknown truck driver usually won't bear fruit.

3. *I violated the principle of searching for a worthy man.*

This trucker was a fornicator. His language was vile, his associates ungodly. It is not surprising he was hostile to the gospel. In a very real sense, I threw pearls to a swine, that which is sacred to a dog. Do swine and dogs get saved? You bet! But it takes a lot more than a quick pass with an evangelistic tool to break up the granite of their hearts.

4. *I didn't know how to minister cross-culturally.*

The trucker's world was vastly different from mine. It was filled with Caterpillar caps, CB radios, Peterbilts, truck stops, Jake Brakes, loose women, tough talk, strong coffee, flannel shirts, and perpetual motion. He worshiped power, sex, pickup trucks, guns, RV vehicles, the open road, and the next woman.

To win the weak, Paul reminded us, we must become weak, throttling back our intellect, holding in check our capacity to wither the heathen with our brilliance and logic. "Becoming weak" doesn't mean joining the lost in their weakness and sin. To win a fisherman, become a fisherman. Learn his language. Enjoy the positive dimensions of his world. Affirm what is of value in his frame of reference. Understand what it takes to capture his attention and convince him of the reality of Christianity. A decision to follow Christ must be made within the framework of his own world, not yours.

5. *It was easier to talk to a stranger than to build a friendship.*

It's always easier to read from a tract than to build into a life. Folks who tell me lifestyle evangelism is a cop-out have never tried it.

In confrontational evangelism, the encounter is scary, intense . . . and brief. Then it's over. Thank God for those who are gifted in such an approach!

Usually, however, these folks don't have to face the issues of separation. Those involved in confrontational evangelism don't spend evenings with the lost where liquor is served, conversations wander, and actions aren't always godly. Seldom do those who go quickly from stranger to stranger know the loneliness of being the only Christian in a group of non- Christian friends. It's embarrassing to be forced to leave a circle of friends and move into another room because the conversation is gross. Furthermore, it's much more difficult to be rejected by a friend than a stranger. The pain lasts a lot longer.

6. *My motives probably were not pure.*

I was new at Dallas Seminary. I had a reputation for being gifted in evangelism. Perhaps I thought it was time to bring a "mouse" to the doorstep. Could it have been a desire for a "quick fix"?

We all have a need to be significant. Sometimes, our desire to be significant is so strong that it compels us to be involved in Christian activities for selfish reasons. I don't always understand my motives.

One thing is for sure. I had no desire to love or serve that trucker. I wanted a clean, antiseptic decision, period. And that's exactly what I got. "No, I'm not interested."

Timing Is Critical

It was Tuesday night. Betty, Jim, Ruthe, and I were enjoying a chicken dinner special at Youngblood's Fried Chicken Restaurant. My truck driver fiasco taught us that methods which worked with college students wouldn't necessarily work in an apartment unit. So we made a tactical shift. We committed ourselves to going out to eat at least once a week with one of our apartment dwellers. This we did for more than four years. Many of these friends came to Christ.

Right in the midst of our finger-lickin' chicken, Betty turned to me and said,

"Joe—Jim and I have noticed something different about you and Ruthe. We're not sure what makes the difference, but we'd like to have it too."

"Happy to talk to you about it some time," I said.

It was clear to me that Betty was ready. Jim wasn't. Therefore, I put off discussing the gospel with them. Why? Our ministry was apartment-wide. It wasn't limited to a specific individual or couple. Jim and Betty knew most of the people in the building. Unlike what I did with my trucker friend, I put off explaining the gospel and delayed trying to get them to a point of decision because:

- I was interested in full-term babies.

- I was committed to the apartment *oikos* and didn't want to jeopardize the larger network.

- I was concerned that if Betty committed herself to Christ first, Jim might reject it. His negative reaction could influence the entire apartment *oikos*. Word spreads, you know.

"But Joe," some of you protest, "Betty was interested *that night*. What if she'd been killed in a car wreck on the way home from the restaurant? You never know when someone will be summoned away from this life, and eternal souls are far too valuable to play with! You've got to strike while the iron's hot! Didn't the apostle Paul say, 'I tell you, *now* is the time of God's favor, *now* is the day of salvation'"? (2 Corinthians 6:2).

Whew! You've got some excellent points there! I'm glad to see that your heart is in entirely the right place. Let me begin by saying that you're both right and wrong.

"Not so fast, brother Aldrich! What do you mean by that?"

I mean that you're right in thinking that *right now* is the appropriate time for people to be reconciled to God. The Lord's offer of salvation is open at this very moment to everyone on earth; accepting that offer *right now* is the wisest and best choice anyone can make.

"That's what I mean! So how can you say it was a good thing that you waited to tell Betty about the gospel?"

Please, let me finish! "Right now" *is* always the best time for someone to come into God's family, but "right now" *isn't* always the best time to *tell* them about God's offer.

"What? C'mon, my friend, that sounds like double-talk to me! How can that be true?"

I admit it doesn't sound compelling when you first hear it. But when you think about it and when you see how highly God values good strategy, it begins to make sense. Stick with me for a moment as we briefly look at a few Scriptures. What all of them have in common, I think, is the value they place on strategy; God puts off or postpones certain good things so that greater things might happen.

Have you ever wondered why God waited until the rise of the Roman Empire to send his Son into the world? Why not send him during Moses' time? Why not earlier, during Abraham's time? Or better yet, why not immediately after Adam and Eve sinned? Wouldn't the world have been spared thousands of years of struggle against sin? The truth is, God had a plan:

> *But when the time had fully come, God sent his Son, born of a woman, born under law, to redeem those under law, that we might receive the full rights of sons* (Galatians 4:4, 5).

> *You see, at just the right time, when we were still powerless, Christ died for the ungodly* (Romans 5:6).

Thousands of Christians also wonder why the Lord doesn't come back today, right now. If it takes God's wisdom and strength to straighten out the world's mess, why doesn't he come now and do something about it? Here's why:

> *I charge you to keep this command without spot or blame until the appearing of our Lord Jesus Christ, which God will bring about in his own time* (1 Timothy 6:13b-15a).

> *He must remain in heaven until the time comes for God to restore everything, as he promised long ago through his holy prophets* (Acts 3:21).

> *And [God] made known to us the mystery of his will according to his good pleasure, which he purposed in Christ, to be put into effect when the times will have reached their fulfillment—to bring all things in heaven and on earth together under one head, even Christ* (Ephesians 1:9, 10).

God's strategy calls for certain things to happen at certain times; not sooner, not later. He postpones certain good things (Jesus' birth, his Second Coming) so that greater things might be accomplished. Jesus followed the same strategy while on earth. This explains some rather perplexing commands he gave in the Gospels:

> While Jesus was in one of the towns, a man came along who was covered with leprosy. When he saw Jesus, he fell with his face to the ground and begged him, "Lord, if you are willing, you can make me clean." Jesus reached out his hand and touched the man. "I am willing," he said. "Be clean!" And immediately the leprosy left him. Then Jesus ordered him, "Don't tell anyone, but go, show yourself to the priest and offer the sacrifices that Moses commanded for your cleansing, as a testimony to them" (Luke 5:12-14).

At another time, Jesus brought a dead girl back to life. What a perfect time for evangelism! Or maybe not:

> Her parents were astonished, but he ordered them not to tell anyone what had happened (Luke 8:56).

Why would Jesus give such commands? One reason involves strategy; if these deeds had been widely broadcast, it would have been much more difficult for Jesus to get around to do the ministry his Father had sent him to do. We don't have to speculate about this. The folks in Luke 5 didn't obey Jesus' command to keep quiet, and here's what happened:

> Yet the news about him spread all the more, so that crowds of people came to hear him and to be healed of their sicknesses. But Jesus often withdrew to lonely places and prayed (Luke 5:15-16).

On at least two occasions, Jesus told his disciples to keep quiet about things they had seen and heard. In Luke 9, when our Lord asked his men about his identity, Peter answered that he was "the Christ of God." The fisherman was right! Wouldn't this be a terrific time to proclaim a mighty message? But Luke says "Jesus strictly warned them not to tell this to anyone" (Luke 9:18-21).

A little later, Peter, James, and John witnessed the Transfiguration, when Jesus appeared in unveiled glory, speaking with Moses and Elijah. The three apostles were overawed. Especially Peter. He wanted to build three lean-tos, one for the Lord and two for his guests, for "He did not know what to say, [he was] so frightened" (Mark 9:6). Don't you think this would be another fabulous time for evangelism? Time's a'wastin'! If you can't get pumped up after a display like that, what would it take? But notice what Jesus said:

As they were coming down the mountain, Jesus gave them orders not to tell anyone what they had seen until the Son of Man had risen from the dead (Mark 9:9).

I'm certain that between the time of the Transfiguration and the day of Pentecost (when evangelism really got going), many people died without coming to know the Lord. Jesus was not unconcerned about these folks; he simply knew that his larger mission would be better served by having his apostles wait before they began proclaiming the Good News. He sacrificed some short-term gains for better long-term results. Paul wrote of the same thing.

For there is one God and one mediator between God and men, the man Christ Jesus, who gave himself as a ransom for all men—the testimony given in its proper time (1 Timothy 2:5, 6).

Paul, a servant of God and an apostle of Jesus Christ for the faith of God's elect and the knowledge of the truth that leads to godliness—a faith and knowledge resting on the hope of eternal life, which God, who does not lie, promised before the beginning of time, and at his appointed season he brought his word to light through the preaching entrusted to me by the command of God our Savior . . . (Titus 1:1-3).

Note that Paul not only believed that God had engineered the timing of Christ's coming, but that he'd arranged the timing even of Paul's own preaching: ". . . *at his appointed season* he brought his word to light *through the preaching entrusted to me.*"

"I think I see what you're saying, Joe, and it does make sense," you say. "But wouldn't it be easy to use 'bad timing' as an excuse never to tell anyone about Jesus? Wouldn't many of us keep quiet when we should speak out, claiming that 'it's just not time yet'? "

Unfortunately, you're right. Let me make one thing clear: I don't want "strategy" or "bad timing" ever to become an excuse for not sharing the Good News when God gives us an open door and a green light. The fact is, the only way you'll know the "right time" is by careful observation and much, much prayer. This isn't a "lazy man's out."

Do you remember how in Acts 16 Paul wanted to evangelize pagan people living in desperate need of the gospel? Here is what Luke records of Paul's missionary trip:

Paul and his companions traveled throughout the region of Phrygia and Galatia, having been kept by the Holy

*Spirit from preaching the word in the provice of Asia.
When they came to the border of Mysia, they tried to
enter Bithynia, but the Spirit of Jesus would not allow
them to. So they passed by Mysia and went down to
Troas. During the night Paul had a vision of a man of
Macedonia standing and begging him, "Come over to
Macedonia and help us." After Paul had seen the vision,
we got ready at once to leave for Macedonia, concluding
that God had called us to preach the gospel to them*
(Acts 16:6-10).

Didn't the people of Asia and of Bithynia (modern-day
Turkey) need the gospel as much as those in Macedonia?
Wasn't Paul at that time geographically closer to Asia
and Bithynia than he was to Macedonia? Why would
God call him several hundred miles away to preach, "wast-
ing" all those days of travel to get there (remember, they
didn't have 747s)?

The answer seems to be that Macedonia was ready,
but Asia and Bithynia were not. Did you notice Paul's
vision? The Macedonians were ripe for harvest—they
were "begging" Paul to come to them. God's strategy
called for Paul to bypass Asia and Bithynia and head to
Macedonia.

That didn't mean God was uninterested in those other
places. In fact, Peter sent his first letter to Christians
who lived in Bithynia (1 Peter 1:1), and early in the
second century the Roman governor Pliny told the Em-
peror Trajan that Christians had established a strong presence in the area. God had a plan for Asia and Bithynia;
Paul simply wasn't part of it.

Note carefully that Paul wasn't looking for an excuse
not to preach to those in Asia and Bithynia. He really
wanted to bring them the gospel! But because he was

deeply and intimately in touch with God and his strategy for bringing people into the kingdom, he knew there was a "right time" and a "wrong time" to do so.

The same should be true of us. *Never* use the notions of "strategy" or "bad timing" as excuses for failing to tell others of Christ when you think God is telling you to speak. Stay in close touch with your Father in heaven. Observe closely your non-Christian friends for signs of readiness. Pray earnestly about what you should do. When it's time, God will guide and empower your evangelistic efforts. That's what he's calling us to do!

By the way, do you know what happened to Jim and Betty? Today, they're both wonderful Christians actively engaged in rearing a Christian family.

I don't know what happened to the trucker.

Reviewing an Effective Strategy for Evangelism

Regardless of our past experiences, what we are doing *now* is what matters. Can you visualize yourself living redemptively in a web of relationships, carefully positioned for maximum impact? What would it take for you to make that a reality? Amos and Zechariah had to work through the same questions.

"Come on Amos, blow out the lamp. It's past bedtime, and I'm zonked."

"Cool it, Zach, I'll snuff it when I'm finished."

"You're 'finished?' What are you 'finishing' this time of night?"

"My diary. I'm keeping a running record of all that has happened. I suspect we may be sent out to do this again."

"Sort of a notebook, huh? I'll bet you're planning

to start a seminar or something and go on the circuit."

"I'm serious, Zach! We're learning some important lessons which I think will help others. No sense in reinventing the wheel."

"So what have you learned? Lay it on me, brother."

"All right, smart aleck, I'll tell you. You'll wish you had never asked."

Can you imagine what lessons our imaginary friends might have learned? Let's review!

1. It's OK to be afraid.

Most of us get butterflies when we consider reaching out into our webs of relationships. It's important to remember we're co-laborers with God, we're adequately armed, and the chariots of fire are but a breath away.

2. Fancy clothes, lots of money, and an elevated position are not necessary.

There's probably nothing wrong with status, power, and money, but there are more significant ways to influence men and women to Jesus Christ. It's usually better to shift our dependence from such things to depending on a different set of dynamics . . . dynamics which grow out of servanthood.

3. It's wise to network with compatible people.

Finding and working with receptive people is at least a good place to begin. All of us have networks. Most of us can easily form some. Within these networks are "worthy" people, men and women of peace.

4. The gift of our need is powerful.

Allowing others to minister to us is a vital part of a genuine friendship, and a significant component of persuasion. It eliminates the temptation to come on as "Mr.

and Mrs. Wonderful" who must be squeaky-clean, totally adequate, virtually perfect, and probably plastic.

5. Accountability is motivating.

Jesus' deployment of two-man teams illustrates the need for communication and accountability. Also encouragement! Evangelism can be tough, tiring, and terrifying. It helps to link up with others of like mind who will be a source of prayer and encouragement.

6. Hospitality helps.

Indeed it does! There's something about breaking bread in a home that knits hearts together. Barriers are broken down, caricatures are eliminated, positive experiences are created, new friendships are formed. Hospitality is not limited to the home— lots can happen in restaurants or cafeterias.

7. Serving communicates.

Nothing seems to be more powerful than a Spirit-filled individual who targets his gifts to meet needs—especially if he has thrown a redemptive switch and experiences the evangelistic impact of a servant lifestyle.

8. Truth must be proclaimed.

Faith is based on what we see and hear. It comes, we are told, by hearing, and hearing by God's Word. Each day, Amos and Zechariah publicly talked about Jesus Christ. They had no formal training. They couldn't even spell *homiletics*. They knew nothing about sermon preparation, and probably didn't own one page of Holy Scripture. They spoke of what they had seen Jesus do and what they'd heard him say. Evenings were undoubtedly spent discussing and debating the message of the day. The goal of all our efforts is that people will hear the gospel and respond to Christ.

9. *Miracles capture attention and verify claims.*

The Lord sent his men to "heal the sick who are there and tell them 'The kingdom of God is near you'" (Luke 10:9). All believers should be living supernatural lives, lives which display divine qualities, deny themselves, serve others, demonstrate the reality of being delivered from darkness into his eternal light, and show the power of the indwelling Christ. A God-flavored person is a walking miracle.

10. *Evangelism is a lifestyle.*

I can't overemphasize this point. Some will "try" lifestyle evangelism for a month or two, then toss it on the pile of other "discarded methodologies." But a tear tumbling down a cheek isn't a "method." Giving two sacks of groceries, then sweaters, hankies, and underwear, isn't a "method." Nor is flying supplies to military bases, networking a Pop Warner football team, or waxing a car. Evangelism is a lifestyle. That means it lasts a lifetime—or it should.

11. *After everything is said and done, more is usually said than done.*

A time comes when it's necessary to act. You can sit on the fence too long. Lewis Carroll had that in mind when he wrote the following lines in *Alice in Wonderland*.

> The Mock Turtle, in a deep hollow tone, said: "Sit down, and don't speak a word 'til I've finished." So they sat down and nobody spoke for some minutes. Alice thought to herself, "I don't see how he can ever finish if he doesn't begin."

Friend, we can't finish if we don't start. Evangelism always starts with a commitment—a commitment, I hope, you have already made.

So where do we go from here?

Tips for Helping People to Christ

I sit here at my computer, wondering what advice to give to someone who wants to become a redemptive neighbor. The question is, "Where do I begin?" Your gifts, resources, and neighborhood may be entirely different from mine. That makes it next to impossible for me to give specifics explaining what you should do. Perhaps the most valuable thing I can do is to make some observations and give a few principles relative to cultivating. Then you can decide where and how to begin.

1. Develop the capacity to draw near.

"Neigh" is the first syllable of "neighbor." "Neigh" and "nigh" are linguistic cousins. They both come from the same root, which can be translated "near in time, space or relationship." To be "nigh" to a city means to be near it. To be a "neighbor" means to be near. Most are neighbors geographically. A few are neighbors relationally. It takes skill to become a neighborly neighbor—we've got to learn it.

We're not naturally neighbors. In fact, to be a neighbor goes against our desire for privacy and security. Yet, the primary factor in "loving our neighbors" is to be a neighbor. To be a neighbor is to develop the capacity to draw near. It involves risk. To be a redemptive neighbor, you

risk rejection

risk censorship from the body of Christ

risk compromise

risk opposition from the evil one

risk misunderstanding by your family and friends

risk a new social schedule

risk new and risky experiences

Take the risk! Think how you'd like to be treated by a neighbor. If you were to list your qualifications for a "Neighbor of the Year" award, what would they be? Would they include any of the following? Would your Neighbor of the Year

be warm and friendly?

have a joyful spirit?

be an open, accepting person?

not be critical or judgmental?

have firm convictions?

be hospitable?

have a warm sense of humor?

have a serving, giving heart?

love your kids?

be sensitive to your needs?

be family-and-home-centered?

be other-centered?

take the initiative in building friendships?

be involved in community activities?

be willing to allow you to help them?

radiate the fruit of the Spirit?

be a worthy, peace-loving person?

be authentic and genuine?

I suspect your Neighbor of the Year would exhibit most of these qualities. Be that neighbor! Look over the list and decide what things you could do to make these qualities become part of your life. Remember, if your non-Christian neighbor sees these qualities in you, he'll take notice.

At the same time, realize that waving all these glorious qualities in front of folks in your cul-de-sac guarantees nothing. Unbelievers often possess many of them. Eventually, you've got to explain how you got them. But get them first! If you don't have them, you'll probably be excluded from having any significant impact.

2. Sign on for the long haul.

Sorry, folks, but that's the way it is. Those lining up in the "cultivators' corner" can expect the hard labor.

Now, God may surprise you by putting a well-cultivated soul in your network. It happens. But soul-culture is costly in both time and resources. I'd love to have a hundred bucks for every meal my wife has prepared for unsaved friends. I'd be delighted to have a dollar for every hour we've spent with non-Christians. I'd be glad to accept a gold bar for every tear we've shed as we've found ourselves woven into the fabric of these dear people's lives.

When you try to influence a whole network of folks in your geographical or vocational network, the magnitude of the task may seem overwhelming. Remember, you're setting a lifetime course. Evangelism is a way of living. You are committing yourself to "stay in that house," to "stick with the troops at the office" as long as you are in that neighborhood or involved in that business. You're not signing on for a quick foray through the countryside. From your perspective, it will probably seem that nothing is happening. Remember Sonya? She had no idea of the miracles God was arranging to coincide with her generosity.

3. *Make contact.*

How can you finish if you don't begin? Evangelism is what spills over when you bump into someone. So bump!

May I be so foolish as to suggest that you must talk, too? That's where it all begins.

"But Joe," you say, "I've lived in my neighborhood thirteen years and haven't done anything."

A businessman in Canada read *Life-style Evangelism* and was convicted that he and his wife had done nothing in their neighborhood for thirteen years. They decided to do something anyway. They just had a new air conditioning system installed, and their next door neighbor was in the heating and cooling business. They invited him and his wife over to celebrate the installation of their air conditioner. Honest to God, it's true.

Over they came. They enjoyed the evening and discovered that their neighbors were delightful people. They continued doing things together for about six months. One day the phone rang.

"Mum and I are planning to go to Hawaii this summer, and we don't want to go alone," their friend said. "As we thought about it, we came to the conclusion that you're our best friends. We'd like you to come with us as our guests."

No kidding! They went and had a wonderful time. The last few evenings in Hawaii were spent in serious discussion about the Lord.

One of the sad discoveries you'll make is that many non-Christians have no real friends. *Sin separates.* You may well be embarrassed by someone suggesting that you are their best friend when you consider the relationship pretty casual. It's happened to me several times. I think to myself, *if you really believe I am your best friend, I hurt for you.* We in the Christian community often take friendships for granted.

If to .be a neighbor is to draw nigh, part of being a redemptive person is to draw them your way. Most folks already have "alive and breathing" contacts—folks at the office, barbershop, gas station, the club, or neighborhood, people who are known on a first-name basis.

What if you're starting from ground zero? Here's a few suggestions:

- Call and make contact.
- If it's appropriate, simply apologize for waiting so long to be neighborly.
- Invite them into your home or apartment.
- Go out for coffee.
- Take a hot pie out of the oven and on the spur of the moment invite them over for pie and ice-cream.
- Be sensitive to their needs. If they're elderly and their driveway is full of snow, shovel it.
- Take them a bouquet of flowers. They're dynamite. Potted plants work well, too.
- Begin the relationship with a fishing trip. It's a great way to get to know folks.
- Ask them about their family, their grandkids.
- Let them help you welcome a new neighbor to the neighborhood.

You know what to do! Why am I telling you all this stuff? Just do it!

4. *Scout out and penetrate their networks.*

One of your goals is to get invited into their world. If you become their friend, they will want you to meet their friends. The goal is to become a genuine friend. Once you get "caught up" in things, you will likely be attending some office and neighborhood get-togethers. You'll meet more and more people. If the Lord chooses to use you to reach a neighbor you have networked, it is quite possible the gospel will flow right past your convert into the network you now share in common.

5. Join already established networks.

They're all around you. Some of them you're already part of—that car pool, or 4-H, or the soccer team. PTA provides lots of contacts. Many service organizations present wonderful opportunities to network and look for "schooling fish." Speaking of fish, how about joining a fishing club, or *Ducks Unlimited*? Have you ever thought about coaching Little League or chaperoning a high school dance?

6. Get involved in a common cause.

How about joining with others in finding food for the hungry, shelter for the homeless? My brother, Jon, pastored a rural church where four-wheel drive rigs were the cat's meow. To these folks, there's nothing more exciting than to get off the road and into the woods. They'll jump at any excuse to head out, especially if they can be of service to others. They like to help. Jon was aware of several elderly couples who needed firewood. He linked some of his own church members with a bunch of guys from the community and roared out to cut wood. Everyone had a ball, and some significant relationships were formed.

Several of us banded together to fight outbreaks of anti-semitism in our community. We took out a full page ad in the Portland *Oregonian*. It involved time, effort, and money.

A Jewish man called me and asked if we could meet

for lunch. He was moved because a few folks cared. We met for lunch. Normally, I don't offer thanks if I'm dining with a nonbeliever, but I felt compelled to do so when Gary and I met. I thanked the Lord that Gary was very special to God, that he had a special place in God's heart. When I finished praying, tears were running down his face. Two weeks later I had the joy of leading him to his Messiah.

7. Keep it simple.

If you entertain, keep it simple. Forget the silver service and crystal. Make it easy for them to invite you back. If you knock yourself out preparing the perfectly-served dinner, they may never reciprocate. Simplicity is the key. Please note that simplicity and sloppiness are not synonymous. Do things well, just don't overdo it.

8. Import lots of humor.

Don't be the Grim Reaper. Loosen up! Smile occasionally! You really weren't weaned on a dill pickle. Don't act that way. Have fun together! Enjoy a good laugh! Yes, you'll have to overlook some of their adjectives. You can't expect a heavenly vocabulary from an earthy tongue. Don't be afraid to laugh at yourself, either. Some Christians take themselves far too seriously. If you're weird, it's not because God made you that way. Pagans think Christians never have any fun. Prove them wrong!

9. Love their kids.

Ruthe and I have thoroughly enjoyed our kids' friends. They are a delight to have around. We consider them our own. Nearly every vacation, we take along someone else's teenager. Try sending these kids with your child to a good Christian camp. It's a great way to reach a family! Make your kids' friends feel welcome. Go out of your way to befriend them. Make an effort to become acquainted with their parents. If the teenagers like you, their parents will know it. And vice versa.

10. Take an interest in their interests.

If antlers hang in their den from floor to ceiling, talk about deer, hunting, guns, and everything in-between. You may be on to something! If you're an expert hunter, don't "top his tales." If you don't know much about hunting, take an interest in it. Ask questions. You won't have any problem making conversation. Don't we all appreciate folks who take an interest in us and our world? May I remind you that friends *listen?*

11. Capitalize on little things.

If he's washing a car, wander across the street and chat for a bit. You could even help out. If she's out on the porch potting plants, walk over and visit. Bring a pot of coffee. Expect to have literally dozens of such "encounters." After all, that's what friends do. The cumulative weight of these encounters builds momentum toward the foot of the Cross. This assumes, of course, that they are positive experiences.

12. Share the gift of your need.

We've talked of this earlier. The relationship must be reciprocal if it's going to be genuine. Significant relationships involve a free flow of resources. You may benefit from their counsel. Perhaps you need someone to help you lift some beams or cut down a tree. Maybe you need to borrow a ladder or a pick and shovel. Perhaps you have a need for forgiveness—you've been very un-Christian in your attitude toward them. Seek forgiveness. Maybe you're going through lots of personal pain. Let them be a source of comfort and help.

13. Anticipate difficulty.

There will be tense moments. You will feel awkward and out of place. At times you will wonder if you are compromising. It's inevitable that you will say too much, and wonder if you have blown it. You may be viciously attacked by a friend; one did that to us. Sometimes a fish fights the hardest when it's closest to the boat. I'm delighted to say that the one who attacked us is now a follower of Christ.

14. Pray every day.

Did you catch that? PRAY EVERY DAY. As you walk, ride, run, or cycle past the homes in your neighborhood or the desks in your office, PRAY. Pray before you do something, pray after you've done it. Believe that God answers prayer, that God prepares hearts, that God works in the huddle and in the hearts of needy people. Pray expectantly. Thank God ahead of time for how he will use you, not just to cultivate, but perhaps to sow and reap.

To do that, you've got to get involved in the lives of lost men and women—and that can get messy. We'll talk about it in the next chapter.

"Comfort zones" vary among Christians.

9

CULTURE VULTURES

"**S**o you don't think Reagan's the answer. Well, if he's not, then who is?"

Even though the pastor was at his first cocktail party, he couldn't pass up the question. He and his wife had become greatly burdened for their neighborhood. Praying for an opportunity to establish some redemptive friendships, they reached out and got invited to a cocktail party.

After much soul-searching, they decided to go. It was a first, a fearsome first. They had no idea what to expect. Three things about the party took them completely by surprise. First, no one got drunk. Second, many just had soft drinks. Third, no one paired off and headed to the bedrooms.

The question about the "answer man" came as the pastor visited with the host around the punch bowl.

"If Reagan's not the answer, then who is?"

"I've got to go with Jesus Christ," the pastor said.

"You're kidding," came the reply. "What makes you think he's the answer?"

As the pastor began to respond, several others crowded around the punch bowl to join the conversation.

"I've never heard this before," the intrigued host said. "Why don't we go sit in the living room and talk about it."

Twenty-one guests assembled in the living room to listen. Christ became the topic of conversation until the party broke up at 1:00 A.M. Within the week, three people called to set up appointments with the pastor to hear more. Within ten weeks, eight folks had found Christ.

Some weeks later, the pastor was pressured out of his denomination for attending the party.

Count the cost, my friend. If you're going to be a redemptive neighbor, you will find yourself on the wrong side of some manmade fences. You may have to wear your Ephesians 6 armor to protect you from other members of the body of Christ.

Staying and Eating

"Stay in that house," the Lord commanded the seventy, *"eating and drinking whatever they give you"* (Luke 10:7).

"When you enter a town and are welcomed, eat what is set before you" (Luke 10:8).

". . . search for some worthy person . . . and stay at his house until you leave" (Matthew 10:11).

The greatest barriers to evangelism usually aren't theological, but cultural. We don't know how to bridge back into the world of the lost. Consequently, we don't want to stay, and we aren't free to eat. Yet, *staying and eating are two of the fundamental keys to effective communication.* Amos and Zechariah discovered this for themselves.

"Amos, how do you think we're doing?"

"What do you mean, Zach?"

"Well, you know, are we doing the job? Would the Lord be pleased?"

"I think so. To be truthful, I guess I thought things would happen a little faster. Maybe I just didn't know what to expect."

"We certainly found a worthy man and a worthy house! I guess if that's part of his strategy, we should get good marks for our efforts. It's opened up the community for us."

"Well, Zach, if we did nothing more than see Isaiah and Mary become followers of Christ, it would be worth it."

"True, but don't forget their family and friends. They're really asking questions, too. Sure makes our job a lot easier!"

"I'm with you on that. Say, what do you think Isaiah and Mary think about all this?"

"I'm not sure, Amos, but I'm certain they were watching to see if we'd eat the meal they prepared for us. I wonder if it was even kosher? You know, old buddy, I think you won Mary over when you complimented her cooking."

"I sensed Mary was a bit nervous about it. But she wasn't the only one."

"Tell me about it! I wanted to pull the shades. I'm still not comfortable with it all. If the Lord hadn't instructed us to eat whatever they put before us, I wouldn't have touched it."

"Well, I can see his point. Why cloud the issue . . . ?"

"Yeah, why get involved in debate over things which take away from focusing on Jesus?"

"Zach, some folks like to mountain-climb over molehills."

"True, Amos. Didn't the Lord say the lifestyle he was introducing was so radical it wouldn't fit in the old Pharisaical wineskins? It would blow them to shreds!"

"A rather loose translation, my friend, but essentially accurate. Those Pharisees have been adding to the law for a long time."

My friends, they still are.

Biblical Rules about Separation

Believe it or not, folks, this is the chapter where I may get into trouble. But that's OK, I'm no stranger to it. My desire is to reflect accurately what Scripture teaches in the area of contact and association with the non-Christian and his world. I'm not especially concerned about hallowing cherished, manmade rules of behavior. What does the Bible say? That's the bottom line.

To be a neighbor, we must "draw near." Motion toward the nonbeliever is crucial to the evangelistic task. Therefore, we must ask what it takes to be "in the world, but not of the world." How do we "stay and eat" without compromise? Is it even possible? Let me develop a few guiding thoughts.

1. Balance salt with light.

Light refers to a saint's inner character made visible through acts of love and service. Fundamentally, light is godliness. To be light demands a commitment to a *radical difference*. Members of God's "Light Team" are pure in heart, hungering and thirsting after righteousness. God's first- stringers practice what they profess. It's practice, not profession, which strips away the proverbial "bushel basket" and allows folks to peek at the treasure in our earthen vessels. Non-Christians need to see the treasure. They need to get *close enough* to see the treasure.

I don't mean that those committed to radical difference are perfect or flawless. Even broken, failing people can be beautiful if they handle their humanity with integrity. A genuine "I'm sorry, will you forgive me?" is a beautiful— and, I might add, unusual—response. If failure is handled in a God- honoring manner, the light is shining. We are certainly more welcome to "stay and eat" if, through the brokenness of our pot, the treasure shines. What counts is a consistent, faithful, godly life.

It's good to remind ourselves that the Lord didn't just sign up anybody who was alive, warm, and breathing. He didn't ask for volunteers. He handpicked his men. Likewise, we don't deploy babes into the wolf pack.

But are we deploying anyone? It seems to me our lights are parked in the pew, our players are benched, we're providing one chalk talk after another. Our mission isn't to warm pews or to compare notes. The huddle can debate nuances of the play only for so long; sooner or later you've got to approach the line of scrimmage and play ball.

We're to put the best that we have on the line for Jesus. Too many folks are walking around with their spiritual umbilical cords unplugged, wondering where to plug them back in. Don't the animal and human king-doms teach us that weaned ones are driven off, that eaglets are tossed out of nests, that children are taken off mom's milk, that believers are to be deployed outward on mission?

A firm commitment to radical difference assures us that those deployed will bring holiness to the heathen. If we don't, our evangelism efforts are in vain. They are also in vain if we don't get to the lost. Radical difference must be followed by *radical identification.* Salty Christians are those in daily, redemptive contact with the lost. If saints attempt to be "salt" with a flickering light, if they compromise, loss of flavor is right around the corner. On the other hand, light without salt— radical difference without radical identification—makes it impossible for the unholy to see what holiness is all about.

2. Anticipate the appearance of evil.

Although the redemptive person is commanded to avoid every *kind* of evil (1 Thessalonians 5:22), he will sometimes find it almost impossible to avoid the *appearance* of evil. Is it any wonder that our imaginary friend Amos wanted to pull the shades? If "kosher's" in, it's tough to swallow that which might be "unkosher," especially if some orthodox brothers are peeking in the window.

(I should pause here for a brief comment on 1 Thessalonians 5:22. The translators of the King James Bible made an error when they rendered the verse, "Abstain from all *appearance* of evil." According to Arndt and Gingrich's *Greek-English Lexicon of the New Testament*—the standard lexicon used by New Testament scholars—the Greek word here (*eidos*) can mean "outward appearance, form," but it can equally mean "kind." The context determines which meaning is appropriate. "Kind" is the meaning the lexicon gives for 1 Thessalonians 5:22, and that's the meaning all modern translations follow.)

Anytime we step over manmade fences, we appear evil to the one who planted the posts and strung the wires. The Lord encouraged his men to ignore the barbed wire of the Pharisees, and he was accused of evil—a false accusation.

When confronted with his alleged "failure," the Lord refused to make his troops "shape up." They continued to harvest on the sabbath and eat with unwashed hands. Had the Lord given in to the demands of the Pharisees, he would have distorted the gospel. Picking grain on the sabbath and eating with ceremonially unclean hands has nothing to do with getting a ticket on the gospel train.

One word of caution: If you're about to jump some fences, make sure the ones you're ignoring were built by man and not by God! God's barbed wire was put there for a reason, and obedient Christians do not go vaulting over it. Make sure you know what you're doing!

3. Avoid unnecessary offense.

Our goal is to be peacemakers. When conflict arises, it should not be because we have been unwise or insensitive in the use of our freedom. Perhaps the only unavoidable conflict would arise out of a situation where I am exercising my freedom in an attempt to be a redemptive person. In other words, if I have to choose between the pettiness of a poorly-informed Christian and a lost soul, I'd best go with the lost soul. I cannot reach the lost and be the prisoner of another Christian's immaturity at the same time. If I'm seen taking a friend to a movie, it's not my problem that my brother doesn't have the same freedom.

4. Expect to be misunderstood.

Those who have never "mixed it up" with the non-Christian community in an effort to be redemptive don't understand. If they've never caught fish in their own back yard, how can they coach you to catch fish in yours?

Some are looking for an excuse to abandon a neighborhood outreach. For others, waving "the appearance of evil" flag is an excellent way to neglect their neighborhood. Such misunderstanding shouldn't surprise us, whether it comes from the lay or the pastoral community. Many have been saved out of the world in dramatic fashion, and suffer from what I call "the peril of the pendulum." They've swung from one to the other extreme, and from this new position become judge and jury for the rest of us. They mean well, but they desperately need balance and stability.

Light needs to be deployed into the darkness. Don't stash it under a peach crate! The Lord said as much.

Unfortunately, a few well-meaning pastors are often the worst offenders. They misconstrue the doctrine of separation and equate spirituality with withdrawal, maturity with isolation, godliness with separation from the world—rather than separation *unto* God. Remember the denominational group which fired the pastor? It's a case in point.

5. Expect to be uncomfortable.

Believe me, you'll want to pull those shades! I'm always a bit ill-at-ease with non-Christians. I suspect the reverse is also true. We're different by nature. Sometimes our very presence reminds unbelievers of their shortcomings, and that's not all bad. Our presence may remind them they haven't been in church or that they are violating some of the basic tenets of the Bible. They sense we can smell sin on them and that we are somehow judging them.

Sometimes we are, and we must. What we hear and see isn't always wholesome, and the only answer is to excuse ourselves. That's an awkward scene, no matter how you slice it. But if we're to remain salt and light, we've got to do it.

6. *Follow your own conscience.*

Resist the temptation to participate in something because another believer's conscience seems to approve of it. *Your* conscience is the critical issue, and since it's only as good as the information it receives, be certain it's biblically informed. If you don't have freedom of conscience to go to a theater, don't go, even though a fellow believer has the freedom. As you mature, God may increase the size of your comfort zone. Perhaps he'll open your eyes to see that many of the limitations we place upon ourselves are cultural rather than biblical.

I taught a class once in Beatenberg, Switzerland, and the ladies who ran the place wore little doilies on their heads. They also didn't drink Coke. Things may go better with Coke here in the states, but not in Beatenberg.

Obviously, I didn't drink Coke in Beatenberg. I drank Apfelsoft, a brand of apple juice. Their consciences wouldn't allow them to find out if "things go better with Coke." Alas, I chug-a-lug the stuff! Since returning to the states, I haven't refrained from Coke because some Swiss sisters can't handle it. They are doing the right thing by limiting their actions to their consciences, but I am not bound by their convictions.

7. *Acknowledge diversity of conscience.*

Some folks can eat food offered to idols, others can't. In fact, two can do the same thing, according to Romans 14, and for one it's sin and for the other it's not. Diversity of conscience explains why. People have varying comfort zones. Listen to Paul:

As one who is in the Lord Jesus, I am fully convinced that no food is unclean in itself. But if anyone regards something as unclean, then for him it is unclean (Romans 14:14).

I've got Baptist feet. Never danced a step in my life. I don't refrain from dancing because of conscience, I just never learned how. If I knew how, I probably wouldn't because of the realties of the Christian community. I have no desire to unnecessarily offend anyone.

I know a wonderful Christian couple, however, who love to dance to live music. As a result, they led a whole dance band to Christ. Last I heard, the group was singing the praises of the Lord in churches throughout the country. Before these band members met this couple and were converted, it's unlikely they ever would have darkened the door of a church. But they're in God's family today because of this husband and wife team.

This same duo started a midnight Bible study on Friday nights for waitresses, bartenders, and bouncers—the "night people." Why target night people? Because before she found Christ, the wife was a cocktail waitress. She understands the world of the late-nighters. Many of these folks have found Christ because this couple has reached out into their world.

It's true that God has granted this couple a larger comfort zone than most. They're convinced that they're doing the right thing, and no verse of Scripture forbids their activities. The folks who sin are those who look down their noses on this couple's freedom. Romans 14 makes it clear that those who do not have such freedom have no right to judge those who do.

The Peter Model

Peter had some problems squaring tradition with the new wine of the Spirit of God. His strong religious heritage made it virtually inevitable that he'd have a run-in with both God and the apostle Paul.

It all started with God's response to the seeking heart of Cornelius, a Roman officer in the Italian Regiment. Devout and God-fearing, "he gave generously to those in need and prayed to God regularly" (Acts 10:2). A devout Gentile, no less!

At three in the afternoon, Cornelius had a vision in which an angel appeared and called his name. Probably in Latin. The angel said:

> *Your prayers and gifts to the poor have come up as a memorial offering before God. Now send men to Joppa to bring back a man named Simon who is called Peter. He is staying with Simon the tanner, whose house is by the sea* (Acts 10:4-6).

If the angel could speak Latin or make himself understood somehow, why didn't he proclaim the gospel himself? His audience was present, accounted for, and certainly ready. If you wanted to impress a Roman brought up on the politics of power, what better way than to speak the Good News through the mouth of a mighty angel? Why put a seeking Gentile on a collision course with a narrow-minded Jew—a poor fisherman, no less?

It's because God's method is to flesh out the Good News. He isn't interested in using an angel to proclaim the gospel to humans. He wanted Cornelius to hear the message of divine grace from a redeemed man who had experienced that grace for himself. He wanted him to rub shoulders with another imperfect human being. He wanted members of two antagonistic parties to come together in love through the gospel.

That's why God didn't tell the angel to leave Cornelius a tract. The angel came to earth so that a Roman might send to Joppa to hear about Christ from a Jew. God sent the angel to give directions, not to proclaim the way of salvation—and that's why he won't send angelic evangelists to your cul-de-sac either.

But back to Peter. The apostle probably was enjoying a little mini-vacation on Joppa Beach. And why not? He probably needed to kick back, soak up a few rays. Nothing like a little sun, sand, and salt air to put things back together again! It's a good thing Peter didn't know Cornelius had dispatched a few servants and a soldier to fetch him. His long-overdue break was about to be cut short.

The next day we find Peter up on the roof, enjoying the cool breeze, the salt air, and the smell of food. Downstairs, a meal was being prepared. In Petrine fashion, the apostle began to pray, dozed off, and had a dream. A large sheet from heaven arrived full of animals, reptiles, and birds. A voice instructed him to "get up, kill, and eat."

The creatures running around in the sheet weren't exactly what Peter had on his lunch menu. You know the story. Peter informed the voice that there was no way he would touch any of the creatures: "Surely not, Lord! I have never eaten anything impure or unclean" (Acts 10:14). The voice rebuked him and said, "Do not call anything impure that God has made clean," v. 15. This happened three times, then the sheet was taken back to heaven. Peter was a slow learner.

Just then the doorbell rang. The plot thickens. "Simon," the Spirit said at that moment, "three men are looking for you. So get up and go downstairs. Do not hesitate to go with them, for I have sent them" (Acts 10:19-20). Peter obliged the heavenly messenger, headed downstairs, and greeted the strangers. "Why have you come?" he asked. The men responded:

> We have come from Cornelius the centurion. He is a righteous and God-fearing man, who is respected by all the Jewish people. A holy angel told him to have you come to his house so that he could hear what you have to say (Acts 10:22).

Then this Peter, a guest in the home of Simon the tanner, "invited the men into the house to be his guests," v. 23. His guests, mind you. It wasn't even his house! Talk about putting your host on the spot!

The Gentiles stayed overnight with Jews. In the same house. Under the same roof. Unprecedented!

Peter violated everything Judaism stood for. You didn't eat with Gentiles. You didn't extend them any kind of hospitality. They were unclean. Everything in Peter's background said, "don't." God said, "do." The story continues.

From Joppa, the little band headed towards Caesarea, the home of Cornelius. When Peter and his companions arrived in Caesarea they were ushered into a home packed with the friends and relatives of Cornelius. True to his frontal nature, Peter didn't dodge the issue:

> You are well aware that it is against our law for a Jew to associate with a Gentile or visit him. But God has shown me that I should not call any man impure or unclean. So when I was sent for, I came without raising any objection. May I ask why you sent for me? (Acts 10:28-29).

There are several lessons to be learned from the case study of Cornelius and Peter.

1. *Both Cornelius and Peter had immense barriers to overcome.*

Make no mistake about it, there was no love lost between Jew and Gentile. Gentiles weren't big on Jews either. At best they tolerated each other.

For God to send Cornelius to a Jew for help complicated things considerably. Both had to reach out and accept the other. Note carefully that it was a divinely-arranged confrontation, one designed to teach subsequent believers how to respond to those who are different culturally, socially, and religiously.

2. *We all need a sheet from heaven.*

Why should we think that only Peter needed a sheet? It's my firm belief that all of us carry excess baggage when it comes to relating to those who are different from us. Have you checked out your sheet? What little creatures are running around in it? I'm sure the sheets of many Christians would be loaded with such ugly little rascals as:

personal prejudices

judgmental attitudes

distorted perceptions of the way non-Christians think and act

negative experiences which must be faced and overcome

unscriptural teachings which distort the gospel and deter the mission of Christ

legalism

fears of all kinds

holier-than-thou attitudes

an inability to minister cross-culturally

nonredemptive priorities

sinful habits and desires

past failures in attempting to bridge back to
the non-Christian

uncertainty

Have you checked your mailbox lately? If God were
to send a sheet to earth with your address on it, what
would it contain? Peter peeked at his sheet three times
before he was willing to change. How many times will
the Lord have to ship you a sheet until you're willing to
rethink your attitudes and actions toward nonbelievers?

3. Peter acknowledged his error.

Once the Lord's message got through, Peter immediately went along with the program. That takes real
maturity and guts. Ahead of him was the possibility of
rejection and censorship. Once he understood God's will,
he flipped a switch and did a one- eighty, despite strong
convictions to the contrary.

4. The Spirit worked in both parties.

The Spirit appeared to Cornelius and headed him toward a rendezvous with an unknown Jew. The same Spirit
woke up a zealous, God-fearing Jew and prepared him to
be hospitable to this seeking Gentile. Peter didn't know
what God was up to; neither did Cornelius. But God
brought a searching heart and a prepared evangelist together.

We seldom see the other side of the coin. We're seldom
aware of what our "unseen partner" is up to. How important, therefore, for believers to be sensitive to the prompting of the Spirit! Note that Peter was praying when the
vision occurred.

Interestingly enough, so was Cornelius. The Spirit told Cornelius, "Send to Joppa for Simon who is called Peter. He will bring you a message through which you and all your household will be saved" (Acts 11:13-14). That same Spirit brought Philip to the chariot of the Ethiopian eunuch and Sonya to a needy stranger. And you to your *oikos*.

5. There is no favoritism with God.

It's good to remember that God has no favorites. How easy it is to conclude that we're on the inside track, that we're God's favorite kids. Not so! Once Peter heard Cornelius describe his vision, he said

I now realize how true it is that God does not show favoritism, but accepts men from every nation who fear him and do what is right (Acts 10:34-35).

After Peter declared the word to Cornelius and his household, the Spirit of God came upon the Gentiles. This was a shocker. There were no Gentiles at Pentecost!

The circumcised believers who had come with Peter were astonished that the gift of the Holy Spirit had been poured out even on the Gentiles (Acts 10:45).

6. The Spirit gave assurance.

When the three servants of Cornelius showed up, Peter declared that "The Spirit told me to have no hesitation about going with them" (Acts 11:12).

When faced with doubtful things, the first order of business is to seek a green light from the Spirit. Where do you look for green lights? Probably the biggest tool of the Spirit is God's Word. He won't lead contrary to it, guaranteed. Neither are we to follow the conscience of someone else. If the Spirit goes to all the effort of communicating with the hearts of both Peter and Cornelius, isn't it logical that he would communicate with us? It's true he probably won't do it as remarkably as he did with Peter and Cornelius—those times called for making a big point that would govern the mission of the church from then on. But he will, somehow, give us assurance.

If a ministry opportunity draws us into gray areas, the first order of business is to get instructions from the Commander-in-Chief. He stands ready to oblige. Often he speaks through the Holy Scriptures. Sometimes he directs through the counsel and wisdom of mature Christian brothers and sisters. But always he'll get his message through.

7. They shared hospitality.

I'm sure the three Gentiles cast furtive glances in every direction when they found themselves in a Jewish home. One wonders what went through their minds. What did they expect? As you recall, a meal was being prepared as Peter prayed and received his vision. The doorbell rang before lunch, and "Peter invited the men into the house to be his guests." They broke bread together. No more sitting in the back of buses, no more Black and White ambulances, restaurants, or restrooms. No more sunset laws. One wonders how God used the hospitality of Simon the tanner in the lives of these men. Undoubtedly it predisposed them to respond to God's grace.

8. To accept your sheet is not easy or automatic.

Peter's experience with Cornelius opened the door for him to dine with Gentiles on a regular basis. He had a new freedom, a larger comfort zone . . . until the big-time Jews showed up. At that point he bailed out on his Gentile friends. Here's the story, as Paul tells it in the second chapter of Galatians:

*When Peter came to Antioch, I opposed him to his face,
because he was clearly in the wrong. Before certain men
came from James, he used to eat with the Gentiles. But
when they arrived, he began to draw back and separate
himself from the Gentiles because he was afraid of those
who belonged to the circumcision group. The other Jews
joined him in his hypocrisy, so that by their hypocrisy
even Barnabas was led astray.*

*When I saw that they were not acting in line with the
truth of the gospel, I said to Peter in front of them all,
·"You are a Jew, yet you live like a Gentile and not like
a Jew. How is it, then, that you force Gentiles to follow
Jewish customs?"* (Galatians 2:11-14).

Paul had to publicly rebuke Peter for his vacillation.
I'm sure Peter protested, "But Paul, I'll offend the Jewish
believers if they see me eating with Gentiles!" Paul's
reply? "Eat with them anyway." He could not allow Peter
to distort the saving grace of God by erecting again the
racial wall that the Cross had eliminated. To have accom-
modated Peter's inconsistency would have compromised
the integrity of the gospel. Peter's memory needed to be
refreshed by another sheet from heaven. Sound familiar?

Gray Area Options

What do you do when you're faced with some "gray
areas"? If you believe your participation in some event
or activity has redemptive potential, and you're sure
Scripture doesn't condemn it, what do you do when
fellow believers look askance at your proposal? One thing
to do is to determine, as best you can, the nature of the
objectors. Let me offer a few descriptions that may help.

1. The professional weaker brother/sister.

A legalist by nature, a "professional" weaker brother/sister has taken the easy way out. First, he/she has settled for a simplistic view of spirituality. He believes the mature believer is the one with the smallest comfort zone. Gray doesn't exist for him; his world is black and white. Second, he thinks you demonstrate spirituality by adhering to a narrow, self-imposed list of "do's" and don'ts." Third, and most serious, all others are expected to conform to this list.

Fourth, this believer is usually a "mature" saint who will not stumble because of the actions of those who reject his petty legalisms. He won't fall into sin because of your deeds; he just doesn't like what you do. Fifth, these folks do more harm than good. They kill joy, resist beauty, and produce ugliness in the name of truth. Many Christians live in mortal fear of such deadpans. Don't! More than anything else, they want to control. Don't let them! They must be confronted in love.

2. The genuine weaker brother/sister.

Folks who are still babes are susceptible to stumbling in the area of doubtful things. We are warned not to put a stumbling block in their path. Children, teenagers, and new believers need careful attention. I think, however, the church as a whole has spent too much time trying to protect our weaker brothers/sisters and not enough time trying to educate them. The weaker brother/sister position is not a lifetime option. It is a developmental period on the way to spiritual maturity.

Susceptible Christians need to understand that they will encounter many within the body of Christ who have lesser or greater amounts of freedom, depending on the issues involved. Once they understand the principle of conscience and the diversity of freedom, they have little excuse to remain a weaker brother/sister. These folks need to be educated. We must not allow them to paralyze our evangelistic efforts.

3. The mature, nonparticipating brother/sister.

These folks limit their liberty for one of two reasons. First, they limit it because they don't have freedom in a particular area. Perhaps they refrain from dancing because they don't have freedom to dance. That is as it should be. Second, they may limit their liberty despite freedom to exercise it. Wisdom has taught them that it is not necessary, and sometimes is not prudent, to exercise all the liberty which is theirs to enjoy. "'Everything is permissible'—but not everything is beneficial. 'Everything is permissible'—but not everything is constructive. Nobody should seek his own good, but the good of others" (1 Corinthians 10:23-24). Depending on the issue, we are probably all nonparticipating brothers/sisters.

4. The immature, participating brother/sister.

This person is not necessarily immature in the sense of lacking in knowledge. His immaturity shows up in his injudicious practice and proclamation of freedom. He/she becomes a champion of liberty and attempts to get others to join the larger circle of his/her conscience. These folks harm the cause of Christ by injuring the lambs.

5. The mature, participating brother/sister.

This individual understands the biblical doctrine of liberty and is balanced and mature in its application. He/she is consistent in applying his/her freedom in Christ. Yet, this person is able to exercise freedom in a quiet, nonthreatening manner which attempts to avoid unnecessary offense.

Sometimes, however, offense is inevitable. Peter must keep on offending the Jews by eating with Gentiles. Mature individuals realize that to be consistent, redemptive Christians, they may have to make some difficult choices. Sometimes our involvement with non-Christians must take precedence over our concern for other believers. These individuals are sensitive to such occasions and do their best to relate effectively to both the Christian and the non-Christian.

The Brown Bag

If you want to become a redemptive person, you'll find yourself struggling with uncharted territory. Your unsaved friends will show up at the door with the "brown bag," and it won't be full of baloney sandwiches.

Believers who follow the John the Baptist model will remind you that John came "neither eating bread nor drinking wine" (Luke 7:33). Certainly he drank liquids, but because he was a Nazarite, we're told he drank neither "wine or other fermented drink" (Luke 1:15). John the Baptist folks will tell you it's off limits, and shouldn't be allowed in the home. John the Baptist folks err not only if they violate their consciences, but if they believe that John the Baptist is the only model for Christian living.

Christ didn't attempt to outdo John the Baptist. He made no effort to be on the far right of the sharply-focused prophet. Those who are trying to model their behavior after that of Jesus will remind us that he said, "John the Baptist came neither eating bread nor drinking wine [but when] the Son of Man came eating and drinking . . . you say, 'Here is a glutton and a drunkard, a friend of tax collectors and "sinners" ' " (Luke 7:33-34).

Apparently what John didn't drink, Jesus drank.

Others saw what he drank, and accused him of being a drunkard. He wasn't a drunkard because he drank wine or a glutton although he ate food. *He was a friend of sinners.*

Every time I speak on the subject of reaching the nonbeliever, the issue of alcohol comes up. And rightly so! It's a part of the social life of many people. I am not going to be a conscience for you, but I will say that you'd better be prepared to handle the brown bag in a biblically accurate, socially acceptable manner. Remember, there will be a diversity of views within the Christian community.

If you have a conscience on this matter, follow it. Don't, however, presume that your view is mandatory for other believers. Remember that the elder is not to "sit long beside the wine cup." If you have liberty, exercise it with wisdom and restraint. If you do not have liberty, exercise your restraint with wisdom. It is not necessary to imbibe to be a redemptive person.

The greater issue is the vast gulf between the world of the mature believer and the unbeliever. We're aliens and strangers in foreign territory. How we bridge that gulf is the key to being a redemptive neighbor. Many of our walls are self-imposed; God hasn't erected them.

May God grant you the desire to check out your "sheet from heaven" and the courage to respond to what you see with wisdom and sensitivity!

The gospel must be clearly explained.

SOW AND TELL

I guess we all have a "when I was a little kid" story. You know how it works. The kids are complaining about having to walk a block in the rain with only an umbrella, coat, and shoes to protect them.

But, of course, when *you* were a kid, it was three miles through rain, sleet, and snow. Oh, you had shoes, all right, but you had to cut out cardboard to fill the holes. That always makes them moan. "Couldn't afford new clothes. Lived off the 'missionary barrel' and hand-me-downs." So it goes.

Well, when I was a kid . . .

My parents, eight siblings, and I lived on a farm. We raised our own food, chopped our own wood, and made our own bread, butter, and cottage cheese. Are you impressed? Hang on, it gets worse. We raised our own beef and an occasional pig or two. We always had a super garden. Our "tractor" consisted of a slightly used horse. You guessed it. Bib overalls and all, there I was, sprig of dry grass in my mouth, barefooted, with both hands on the plow, turning over the sod.

My kids leave the room at about this point. City-slicker teenagers just don't appreciate the finer things of life.

How can I forget the smell of fresh sod turning over, a sweaty horse, the warm, moist soil between my toes, the unearthed worms trying to get re-buried before being discovered by a persistent blackbird?

Once the soil dried, it was time to plant. The corn planter was filled, squash hills prepared, bean poles put in place, and the seed delivered to its proper location. I get jazzed just thinking about it! We reaped in the fall what we planted in the spring. If we cultivated, weeded, watered, and fertilized well, we had an abundant harvest.

We always cultivated with a view to sowing and reaping. A farmer'd starve to death if he just cultivated. He might have the most beautifully-prepared soil in the valley, but if somewhere along the way, at the right time, he didn't plant seed, he'd wind up with the prettiest, most useless soil in the valley. And everyone would call him a fool.

Enough of the little parable! Got the point?

Sowing Saints

God sows saints (beautiful seed) to cultivate, sow, and reap. If evangelism involves "show and tell," cultivating is "showing." It is revealing the universals of God's character through the particulars of everyday living. It's buying groceries, sweaters, hankies, and panties. It's fixing a stranger's car on your day off or cheering on a losing team or loaning a lawnmower. But none of these things by themselves will ever get a person to heaven.

Ultimately, faith comes by a careful examination of the facts. A solid faith is based on reliable data, data which can be both observed and assimilated from formal or informal communication. You've got to sow the Word in the ears of the lost.

Cultivating demonstrates, sowing declares.

Cultivating appeals to the heart, sowing to the mind.

Cultivating is visual, sowing is verbal.

Cultivating prepares, sowing presents.

Cultivating bonds, sowing explains.

Cultivating shares experiences, sowing explains them.

Sowing draws from two major data banks: Personal experience and propositional revelation. Your bio and the Book, if you will. You sow when you explain how Christ has blessed your life. You sow when you give a book, a tract, a verse of Scripture, a film, or a tape which addresses a need or develops a biblical idea.

I think it's about time we checked in with Zechariah and Amos, our two old buddies. They're nearing the end of their assignment. How do you think they feel about their progress?

"You getting lonesome, Zach?"

"Sorta. The Pony Express strike hasn't exactly helped. We haven't gotten any news from home in a long while! Hope Deborah's doing OK."

"Well, I'm the same way. I've been encouraged, though, by looking through my diary. Zach, my friend, we're doing OK."

"I agree with that. Did you notice Mary's response to what you said last night? I think you really got through to her."

"Hope I didn't say too much."

"Hey, Amos, take it from me. You didn't! She was

with you all the way. I think she could really identify with your background and the struggles you went through when you lost your boy. Not to mention the bitterness."

"Well, if God can use my pain, I guess that's a good thing."

"You know, it amazes me that when we're real, when we don't sugarcoat things, people listen. I don't think she's listened since they lost their daughter. She needed to hear that you were bitter toward God and how he changed you. She needs what you've got!"

"And I think she really wants it, Zach! Probably never believed she could be at peace again."

"And be forgiven. That's got to be a big one! I thank the Lord I learned some Scripture when I was a kid. It's come in handy on several occasions."

"You do well with Scripture, Zach—they pay attention. I think they respect someone who speaks right up. And you're not bossy or anything. I appreciate that."

"Like Jesus said, timing is important. I don't think we could have gotten away with it when we first came. But doors are opening. I really think we're planting some good seeds."

The Principles and Practice of Sowing

Since this is the last chapter, it's time we started wrapping up. Let's take a look at some good, basic principles pertaining to effective sowing.

1. Sow on cultivated soil.

We've talked much about this. Good seed does best when it is buried in good soil. There's no sense in casting good seed to dogs or swine, on packed paths or in thistle patches.

2. *Keep the birds away.*

The robber birds hear the seed hit the soil and come in swarms. Cults are knocking down lots of doors. When your neighbors get targeted, don't stand by and let them be led to slaughter. A few carefully placed comments may be all it takes to steer them away from enslavement to the lie. Christian bookstores have excellent materials to help you with cults.

3. *Sow compatible seed.*

Soils differ. Some plants thrive in soil that kills other plants one row over. A scientifically inclined individual might be moved to respond to Christianity by reading a well-written book on the creation/evolution controversy. Dr. Graham's best-seller, *Peace with God*, might open the door of another's heart. An interest in the future can provide an open door for a good book on prophecy. Family concerns make the James Dobson film series a good sowing tool. Chuck Swindoll's books can have great appeal for the right person.

4. *Space the seeds properly.*

A hill of corn usually does best with three seeds. You won't get a good crop if you pour a dozen or so in one hole. If you can visualize each seed that "registers" as a divine nudge toward the Cross, it may help you understand the process of sowing spiritual seed. Our goal is for truth to register, not simply to be "scattered." Better to communicate a little with high comprehension, than lots with little comprehension. It may be a word of testimony this month, an interesting tract/article the next month. Taking in a Christmas concert may be a great follow-up planting. Why not start an annual neighborhood Christmas party?

5. Sow a diversity of seeds.

Visualize yourself as a seed planter, injecting divinely turbo-charged truth into lives over a period of time. Anticipate continued contact, and don't use the same "seed" for every planting. Books, tapes, comments, concerts, banquets, etc., are all ways to focus your cultivation efforts toward the Cross. When you're fishing with a buddy, you're cultivating. When you comment about the beauty of the stream and the wonder of your Lord's handiwork, you're sowing. If you clean his fish, you're cultivating. If you talk about the big fisherman, you're sowing. A plant, a card, or hot piece of pie is cultivating. (If it's apple pie, it's heaven.)

6. Back up sowing with cultivation.

Soul culture is a bit different than most agriculture. In soul culture, one often sows and cultivates at the same time. It is cultivating that gives sowing its power.

A godly life prepares one to listen to God's Word.

A godly life reinforces the Word of God.

A loving heart opens a hard heart to the heart of God.

A sacrificial act directs one toward the sacrifice.

A friend of mine trusted Christ because a buddy of his loved him, spent time with him, and kept after him. Forty-six times this man asked my friend to go to church or to participate in some church activity. Each time he declined. On the forty-seventh invitation, my friend went and received Christ. He is now in full-time Christian service.

7. Anticipate a cumulative effect.

Read the previous paragraph. What more can I say? It is important for you to visualize a cumulative approach, believing that every word of testimony, every tape, book, or tract creates momentum, especially when backed with a godly life and tons of prayer. You're reprogramming an experience bank of one who probably has more negative data than positive.

8. *Expect a counter-sowing*.

It isn't only in the realm of physical science that there is an equal and opposite reaction for every action. When God the Father sowed as recorded in Matthew 13, an enemy came and sowed weeds in the same field. It's often "two steps forward, one step back."

Sometimes it's the other way around. The wolf protects his pack. He'll tempt you to give up. A conflict will develop. Your kid will get in a fight with someone in the family you're trying to reach. You'll get discouraged. The neighbor's dog will bless you with his calling cards. Smile! It may get worse.

9. *Sow at the proper time*.

Don't sow on company time! Don't be the watercooler warthog. Nobody wants to be accosted at the counter, either. If you're not up to par, if you don't work hard, if you're lazy or sloppy, then cool it on the evangelizing. Better to say nothing than to say something and be the laziest guy in the shop. Back up your lip with your life, or keep it zipped. Don't let your mouth write a check your body can't cash! For Christ's sake, be the best employee you can be. Earn a platform from which to make the gospel clear.

10. *Share your sowing*.

Cross-pollinate your *oikos* with other believers. After you've determined the interests and concerns of your seeking friends, link them with other resources. Others can plant seeds in the garden of your friends' hearts. Expose them to Christians who model joy, holiness, and creativity. Invite them to activities and events which will expose them to others who live to the glory of God. This exposes the seeking person to the variety of ways God works in the lives of his children.

11. *Speak with the expectation of harvest.*

Your attitude, your whole demeanor, will be different if deep in your heart you are expecting that you or someone else will have the joy of reaping. You'll be halfhearted if you expect no results, if you consider your efforts futile. You may not reap. That's OK! But pray that you might do so. Pray that God will use one of his numerous means to "give the increase."

12. *Anticipate receptive periods.*

People are especially open during significant lifestyle changes, such as the death of a loved one, marriage, the birth of a child, a new job, or retirement. A sensitive, available Christian can use these events as avenues for communicating the gospel. It doesn't hurt to remember important anniversaries either.

13. *Sow quality seed.*

No junk! Forget the cheapie, ugly tracts. Anything associated with Christ should be quality, whether a book, tract, tape, or film. Stick pins and bumper stickers aren't going to win our world. Don't be stingy when it comes to communicating the Good News of Jesus Christ. Remember, the medium is the message.

14. *Prepare the crop for harvest.*

At Aldrich Acres, it was always a race to get the hay into the barn before the rain baptized it. Once the sickle bar did its work, it was panic time. We knew we only had a window of a couple of days. We'd check the weather, cut, and windrow it. The moment it was dry, we hired someone to bale it, and then hustled it into the barn—most of the time before it got soaked. Lots of work preceded harvest. Spring meant fertilizing. Summertime we irrigated. All these activities looked forward to "harvest." That's what it's all about.

Granted, you may not be the reaper, but you can network your *oikos*, those seeking friends, with someone who can. If you are fortunate to have an evangelist in your church or community, often that gift is what God uses to reap the souls who have been carefully cultivated and planted. Most who go forward at a crusade meeting have been brought by a friend.

15. *Speak with the expectation of joy.*

Remember, "the seventy returned with joy." God gave the increase. Lives were touched, victories won. Those who go out weeping will return with joy.

Declaring the Words

A woman in Colorado read *Life-style Evangelism* and called to tell me that she and her husband decided to start cultivating and see what happened. They weren't, she assured me, reapers. This dear couple singled out some "worthy folks" in the husband's business network (*oikos*). One woman seemed to be particularly responsive.

This couple went to work, and several months later I got a letter full of superlatives, punctuated with exclamation points, overflowing with joy. This non-reaping couple had just won their first convert.

Their seeking friend had told them of the hurt and pain in her life. The couple listened and loved. Then one Sunday afternoon this hurting woman called and said she had to talk. The Christian lady found herself grabbing her Bible, going to the woman, and leading the lost soul to her Savior. The "reaper" was ecstatic. "I never dreamed," she said, "that I'd ever reap."

As you know, reaping isn't easy. It's the "sweaty palms" phase of evangelism. Although much could be said, I'm not going to develop "Declaring the Words" in great detail because I covered it in *Life-style Evangelism*. Furthermore, this book is targeted for you cultivators and sowers. But because many of you will become reapers, I'd like to help you move into that mode with ease and grace. Let me give you some encouraging thoughts about reaping.

1. It's a great joy to help a friend receive Christ.

Emotions run high when new birth takes place! I made a serious attempt to sell life insurance when I was in college. "Attempt" is probably the appropriate term, because it wasn't much more than that. More often than not, I ended up declaring Christ as the ultimate life assurance.

I'll never forget the evening I led my boss to Christ. He opened up his life to me and spilled out his heart. Although a wealthy man, things weren't going well. He pulled his brand new Chrysler 300 over to the curb as we started talking about spiritual things. "Joe," he asked, "if you were me, what would you do?" I said, "Mr. Carrigan, I'd commit my life to Christ." I was shaking like an aspen in a wind storm. But I've never forgotten the sheer joy of praying with him as he received Christ.

2. A friendship often sets the stage for reaping.

I would not be surprised if most people who are diligent in cultivating and sowing discover themselves reaping. Full-term babies often pull the information out of you. It is therefore important that you know how to "put in the sickle."

3. Reaping is more effective if the presentation is clear.

The "no method" folks need to realize that "no method" *is* a method . . . usually a poor one. It's true that millions found Christ before there was a "Four Spiritual Laws" booklet, but God has used that little tool to lead many to Christ. I use the "Four Laws" myself. You might prefer "The Bridge," or "Steps to Peace with God," or the *Evangelism Explosion* materials, or the "Roman Road." The particular method doesn't matter too much. It's important, however, to recognize several advantages of using methods.

   a. They are logical in their approach. In other words, they are designed to lead to a point of conclusion. Each principle builds upon a previous one.

   b. They focus attention, allowing you to be in charge of the conversation. The listener expects that you are going to move through the entire presentation.

   c. They provide appropriate Scripture references. This is particularly helpful if you don't know them.

   d. They keep you on the topic. Random conversations make it easy to detour into all the questions and excuses which Satan seems to bring to mind. A specific presentation avoids a lot of these unnecessary questions. If asked about "the heathen in Africa," a structured presentation allows you to suggest that you finish the presentation, and if the question is still a concern, it will be addressed.

   e. They can be personalized. I don't read from the "Four Laws" booklet. I write it out—the teacher in me enjoys that. Furthermore, the presentation becomes "custom made" and can be adapted to different backgrounds and understanding. If they don't know much about who Christ is, you can spend more time on Law Three. Writing out the presentation also provides seekers with a spiritual document which often becomes very special to them. Date it and give it to them after they've received Christ.

f. They build your confidence. A plan, a workable method, makes communication easier. You're more apt to initiate conversation about receiving Christ if you are confident you have an effective method you are comfortable with.

4. Reaping may involve others.

We've already talked about blending gifts to reach the lost. If Billy Graham is coming to town, start cultivating immediately so that you can hitchhike on his gifts. Be one of the thousands who will bring a friend, and rejoice in seeing new life come through God's use of an evangelist.

5. Pray for the opportunity to reap.

I know, it sounds like I'm contradicting myself. Cultivators cultivate, and reapers reap, right? Almost right. I want you to have the joy of reaping. You've done the hard labor, why not pray for a taste of the reaper's joy? At least pray about it. Pray for open doors. Pray for boldness. Pray for an Apollos to water and that God would give the increase. Ask God to burden your heart with some people in your *oikos*. Pray every day for them. God will honor your prayers.

6. Speak with your normal voice.

If God gives you the privilege of telling someone the Good News, don't kick into a religious twang or a stained-glass voice. The Holy Spirit doesn't need it. Talk like you talk when you're discussing the Super Bowl or your favorite recipe.

7. Know when enough is enough.

If you sense that the person is resisting your presentation, it may be a signal to back off. Effective communication is not based on how much you say, but upon how much is received. Sometimes it's smart to change the subject, believing that the individual has received enough for the moment.

8. Anticipate some opposition.

Expect that the doorbell will ring, the phone will jangle, and the baby will start crying. It's spiritual warfare, my friend! The evil one will do all he can to subvert, interrupt, and raise objections.

9. Use gentle persuasion.

In the light of Satan's attempt to abort your whole presentation, don't hesitate to apply some loving pressure; nudge a bit. By and large, people want you to make a decision for them. They expect to be encouraged to act. Yet, people want to buy, not be sold.

10. Stockpile resources.

Have on hand a supply of "Four Laws" booklets or whatever you find helpful. Also, be on the lookout for well-done tracts, booklets, tapes, and music. I've been impressed to see how God can use a well-done musical tape. People enjoy listening to it and don't feel that they are being "evangelized." The music penetrates deep into their hearts. One neighbor told me, "I feel good inside when I listen to your tape. I don't feel that way when I listen to mine." Interesting!

11. Discover or develop some harvest vehicles.

The peaches must get to the processing plant, and

there are lots of steps from the tree to the shelf in the grocery store. If reaping doesn't seem an option for you, perhaps you can construct some harvest events which would impact your *oikos*. Let me suggest a few.

a. Bring an evangelist to town. It may seem impossible, but God specializes in doing the impossible.

b. Join with other believers to sponsor a Christian concert at a local civic auditorium. Invite your neighbor or friend.

c. Help sponsor an evangelistic breakfast where a prominent individual declares his/her faith. Many will go hear an athlete or some other person of accomplishment.

d. Arrange for the showing of a need-centered film series. Anything by Chuck Swindoll or James Dobson would be excellent. Check with your local film library.

e. Invite your friend to a seasonal celebration, such as a fall family festival, a Christmas concert, or an Easter service. If your church doesn't have one, volunteer to put it together.

f. Bring them to a healthy church. God isn't going to put healthy babies in a diseased incubator, so if your church isn't healthy, reject this option.

g. Take them to a weekend retreat at a Christian conference center. Help plan a weekend event for non-Christians. Ruthe and I saw some wonderful results from this kind of activity. Plan on lots of fun!

h. Start, sponsor, or participate in an evangelistic

home Bible study. Underline the word "evangelistic", i.e., specially designed and targeted for non-Christians. Most home Bible studies are *not* properly focused for evangelism. *Life-style Evangelism* has further discussion on the essentials for an effective evangelistic study.

i. How about a personal Bible study? Plan a regular time when you and your friend can work your way through the Gospel of John. God's Word is powerful!

12. Expect results.

When you speak the words of the gospel, expect that the individuals listening will respond. Give them clues as to your expectation: "Jim, when you make this commitment . . . " Anticipate that your "silent partner," the Holy Spirit, is in control of the situation. You're not alone.

Expecting results is not the power of positive thinking, it's faith. It's believing that God has burdened you for the individual, that you've been praying, and the door is opening. Expect God to work. If the individual is reluctant to respond at this juncture, don't give up. It's probably a matter of readiness and timing.

13. Relate your own experience of Christ.

Woven into your gospel presentation should be the "people benefits" of knowing Christ. What things are real to you? Don't pump sunshine or come across "problem free" since the day of your conversion. Speak candidly and honestly from your experience, especially if it relates to what you know of your lost friend and his/her experiences.

14. Anticipate objections.

The advantage of speaking about Christ with friends is that you know them and their background and can anticipate their concerns. This is where you "tailor make" your presentation to fit them and their circumstances. If you're a wise vacuum cleaner salesman, you don't demonstrate rug cleaning capabilities to a woman with wooden floors.

15. Know how to close.

You must ask for the order. It is particularly important to know what you are going to do when you approach the time for response. I usually ask three questions:

a. Does this make sense?

b. On the basis of this (the "Four Laws" presentation) do you feel you have ever committed your life to Christ?

c. Is there any reason you would not want to receive Christ right now?

Notice that the third question does not ask if the person wants to. It asks if there is any reason why the friend wouldn't want to. If a person is going to reject Christ, I want to know why.

16. Provide assurance and follow-up.

Once your friends have prayed to receive Christ, it is a good idea to review some of the basics.

a. Explain again what they have done.

b. Ask them questions to determine their understanding of what they have done.

c. Go over key verses to provide assurance.

d. Encourage them to be involved in some follow-up activities. Who could better do that than their spiritual parents?

e. Get them into a good local church.

f. Continue to be their friend, and introduce them to your friends.

The main thing is to get their mind focused on Christ, what he has done, and their relationship to him. Successful evangelism always focuses on Christ. You might talk about any number of things to get people to Calvary, but once you're there, you've got to talk about who's nailed on that Cross and why.

Farewell to Amos and Zechariah

It wouldn't be right to end this book without an exit interview between Amos and Zechariah and their hosts. Our two drafted evangelists have put into practice the methods of Jesus, they've seen the wisdom of his strategy. Do you think they're satisfied with the results?

"Well, friends, what do you think? Do things look OK? Will Jesus be pleased?"

"Mary, you've done a super job! Jesus is going to love your house. Seriously, it looks smashing."

"Yes indeed, Mary, you've really got talent. That bouquet of wild flowers is frosting on the cake. The colors are spectacular!"

"Isaiah picked them for me. They do add a nice touch."

"Jesus will notice them, Mary. Believe you me! He loves nature and God's creation."

"Isaiah, he'll appreciate your furniture, too. You know, he was quite a craftsman himself. I've watched him respond to quality workmanship. I'd be willing to bet he'll run his hands over that chair you made. It'd be just like him to do that. He notices those kinds of things."

"I worked hard on that one, Amos! It's tough to get good lumber these days. I hope Jesus likes our home! Be honest with me, boys. Do you think he'll like us? We're just ordinary folks."

"Oh, Mary, Isaiah, he'll love you! When Jesus walks in here this afternoon, you're going to be the happiest people in town. Honestly, there isn't a person in this world I'd rather introduce you to than my friend, Jesus."

"Well, let me tell you we're excited about meeting him! We don't know how to say 'thank you' for getting us on his schedule. If he's what you say he is—and judging from your lives, he must be—then the sooner he gets here, the better off we'll be. Thanks so very, very much, my friends!"

"The pleasure's all ours!"

That's enthusiasm, folks! Is that how you feel? You know, as tough as evangelism can be, it's worth it all when you see someone fall in love with Jesus.

Why Get Involved in Evangelism?

You don't get involved in evangelism because you feel guilty. You don't get involved in evangelism because it's your duty. You don't get involved in evangelism because someone makes an emotional appeal, complete with sobering charts and grim statistics.

Do you know why you get involved with evangelism? You get involved because Jesus is a pearl so precious that a man would sell everything he owned in order to get it. You get involved because Jesus stretched out his arms in love on the Cross to draw to himself his lost sons and daughters. You get involved because Jesus is the King of kings and Lord of lords, the Rose of Sharon, the Lamb of God, the Prince of Peace, and our great treasure.

My friend, once you fall in love with this Jesus, you will do everything in your power to introduce others to him. You might not be a reaper; so cultivate! Make up your mind to do whatever you can to help your friends and acquaintances come to know and cherish the Savior. He's a wonderful, magnificent, glorious, loving Lord, and he's asking you to join him in his harvest field.

Let me end this book with a hymn of praise that the apostle Paul—who spent his life introducing people to Jesus—sang in Ephesians 3:20-21. Let it be the expectation of your heart and an encouragement to your soul.

Now to him who is able to do immeasurably more than all we ask or imagine, according to his power that is at work within us, to him be glory in the church and in Christ Jesus throughout all generations, for ever and ever! Amen.

Evangelism is front-line spiritual warfare.

TWENTY-FIVE FREQUENTLY ASKED QUESTIONS

Certain questions about lifestyle evangelism crop up whenever I'm asked to speak on the topic. The following questions are among the most frequently asked. I deal with many in greater detail elsewhere in this book, but I offer the following as a brief, handy guide to some critical issues about using your gifts and interests as mighty tools for evangelism.

1. Doesn't an evangelistic strategy suggest a canned approach to reaching people?

On the surface, yes. Ultimately, however, strategy is simply your best effort at finding out how your abilities mesh with God's redemptive purposes and how they can become productive in God's service. Good strategy collects and analyzes data about yourself and your giftedness, and helps you develop a reasonable plan for the productive use of your God-given abilities.

2. Do you oppose the use of methods such as Evangelism Explosion and other door-to-door strategies?

Not if those involved are gifted in such harvest strategies, and certainly not if men and women are finding Christ through them! I recognize, however, that most of us aren't gifted in such methodologies, and as a result we become frustrated when we try to employ them to influence folks for Christ. Discovering that evangelism is primarily a way of living opens the door for many more of us to get involved significantly in the evangelism process. Soul culture is a joint venture!

3. *Are you sure evangelism involves feeding the hungry and clothing the naked—that is, in meeting the physical and social needs of people?*

Isaiah, Jesus, Paul, Peter, and James certainly seemed to think so. Now, certainly we can't stop with meeting people's physical needs; but if serious needs exist, it's a marvelous place to begin! The testimony of most people who come to Christ includes someone who loved them in very tangible ways.

4. *Do you think every Christian should be involved in lifestyle evangelism?*

No, not if they're not "living the life." Even so, remember that every Christian, mature or immature, holy or carnal, is a living epistle being watched and evaluated by outsiders.

Only a Spirit-filled believer qualifies to give himself away in service to others. Many believers are not mature enough to involve themselves in significant, redemptive contact with unbelievers. Many more are mature enough, but aren't doing it. Some, because of age or other limitations, are not able to befriend non-Christians.

5. *Can a decision to "flip a redemptive switch" really make a difference?*

Absolutely! Christians who flip the switch see the nonbeliever with a new set of eyes. They recognize the joint-venture partnership between themselves and God and believe that the Lord is delighted to use their gifts and abilities. They believe God can use the most insignificant encounter with a nonbeliever. They become seed planters with long-range vision.

6. Shouldn't we be leading people to Christ as soon as they show interest?

This question often comes from someone concerned about the possibility of Jesus returning before an unsaved friend trusts Christ. It's a legitimate concern.

Let's suppose you have befriended five people, two of whom are among the elect. The Lord's coming in three weeks. What's your responsibility? Your job is to love those neighbors, praying each day for boldness and open doors. Pray that you or another might lead them to Christ. Before the three weeks are up, God will either answer your prayer by allowing you to lead them to him or will use another believer as the reaper.

Christians fail because they are not building relationships, because they're not loving and praying daily for the lost. If you are in step with God's Spirit, he will show you the appropriate time and manner in which to make the gospel plain to your friends. The trick is to stay in close touch with God and his agenda. That's hard work, I won't kid you—but the rewards are more than worth it.

7. I don't consider myself mature enough to share Christ. I'm not sure I am ready.

Who's ready to get married? If you waited until bride and bridegroom were ready, it'd be too late. The Bible says to "let our *progress* be made known to all men," not our perfection. How we deal with shortcomings in our lives is often the key to effectiveness in our evangelistic efforts. Sometimes it's good for your neighbor to see you blow it. How you handle failure may convince him you've got something real. The worst thing you can do is to fake it, then to become sanctimonious. The very word *sanctimonious* sounds ominous. Prudes won't cut it, neither will hypocrites or do-gooders.

8. Why don't we just preach? Don't lots of the cult folks look real good?

They sure do. That's why "looking good" isn't enough. The Egyptian magicians could imitate Moses . . . up to a point. So can the cults imitate much of Christianity. That's why "walk" isn't enough. But if "walk" backs up the "Word," we have a two- edged sword. To be saved, people must be convicted by the Spirit of sin, righteousness, and judgment. There really is a difference between goodness and godliness. The two are not synonymous. One can be "good" and yet not godly. Ultimately, the issue between those who look good and those who are good is truth. People need to "hear the words" to become true saints.

9. Is lifestyle evangelism the only strategy for the whole church?

Yes and no. In areas where no church is established, the approach to evangelism must often be more proclamational and confrontational. Once the church is established, evangelism strategy becomes more personal and relational. The lives of believers become a key factor in reaching lost friends.

10. Why do so many Christians have little redemptive contact with non-Christians?

Many are confused concerning the doctrine of separation, and have distorted ideas about the non-Christian community. In Scripture, separation is primarily and fundamentally a separation *unto* God. Those "separated unto God" are not likely to be compromised by association with nonbelievers.

We are not to lose our visibility as lights or our flavor as salt. Contact can lead to compromise; it is a very real possibility. In a war there are casualties. Obviously we want to minimize the number of casualties, but not by withdrawing from the war. Even well-trained, highly-skilled soldiers get wounded.

Furthermore, many Christians are afraid of non-Christians. They don't know what to say, do, or how to act in their presence. Often they perceive them as the enemy. They're not. They're the victims of the enemy. Our job is to rescue those we can, and you can't rescue someone with whom you have no contact.

11. I attend a "separatistic" church. I agree with your thesis that evangelism is a lifestyle, but if I reach out to non-Christians, I will face strong opposition from my church. What should I do?

That's a tough question! Biblically, you should use your gifts and abilities to reach the lost. Evangelism is not primarily fishing in the stained glass aquarium. Become an "undercover" evangelist and start doing what God says: "Love your neighbor." Wouldn't it be better to win someone to Christ and get kicked out of a church than to follow the church and abandon a lost neighbor? Challenge some of the church leaders to reconsider their culturally-defined concepts of evangelism!

12. Should I sit in bars, waiting for contacts to befriend for Christ?

I wouldn't. I really don't think that's the place to meet potential converts. If you're made of dynamite, don't stoke blast furnaces. Am I saying that a Christian should never go into a bar? I didn't say that either. A desperate friend may call you and ask you to meet in a bar. Many Christians would have freedom to do that. You may not. If you don't, *don't.*

13. If I become a sheep, I'll lose my job.

You might. Remember, though, that sheep aren't meek and weak. They're powerful. To be a Christian doesn't mean we're called to roll over and play dead or to be milquetoast Marvins. Be the best employee you can possibly be. Be at the top of the production charts, become a valued employee with a servant's heart. Who can fight that? Who would want to fire that?

14. My wife doesn't have the gift of hospitality, so use of our home as a redemptive tool is out.

Maybe. Maybe not. Perhaps you've convinced her that to entertain folks she's got to put out a five-star meal with live entertainment. Hamburgers are better. If she burns boiling water, bring a pie home and slop some ice cream on it. The neighbors will love it. Furthermore, all "entertaining" doesn't have to center in your home. Nor does it need to focus around food. Go waterskiing together, or fishing, hunting, sailing, or rent a balloon. Perhaps your primary *oikos* will be your place of employment.

15. I don't have time to do all that you are suggesting. What do I do?

Granted, this takes time. But if you're going to be involved in your daughter's soccer games anyway, why not network that group and kill a couple of birds with a single rock? Utilize "influential moments." Walk across the street and visit for a moment or two. You never know what may develop. Furthermore, don't be in a rush. Hang in for the long haul. Rearrange your social schedule to include your neighbors and friends.

16. My house is nothing fancy. Can God still use me?

You bet your army boots! A real person is a whole lot better than a house full of expensive furniture inhabited by a neurotic super-saint. Be real, be genuine, be warm, be yourself. God regularly uses that which is simple to confound the "wise."

17. My neighbors are dangerous. Should I still try to reach them?

Those who are vile or violent are probably not candidates for you to win to Christ. Pray, definitely! But if they are a threat to you and your family, probably you should not attempt to build bridges to them. Remember the dogs and swine. Don't feed them.

18. I'm afraid of people. What do I do?

There's no growth without risk. A Dale Carnegie course might help; many have discovered new confidence through such a program. It may be that the most significant contribution you can make is to ask the Lord of the Harvest to thrust forth laborers. That's a major contribution!

19. My husband's not a believer. Should I still be involved in evangelism?

Yes, if possible, but probably not at home. Don't become something he resents. He doesn't want a "Bible lady" at this point in his life. Perhaps your personal circle of friends can become the focus of your ministry.

20. How do I get my church interested in lifestyle evangelism?

Talk to your leaders. Get them a copy of *Gentle Persuasion* or *Life-style Evangelism*, or of some other good resources which help them understand that evangelism is a way of living.

21. What if I blow it?

You probably will! It's better to swing, hot or cold, than not to swing at all. God can pick up after us and often turns "failures" into "successes." If you offend a neighbor or friend, seek forgiveness, make restitution. How you handle failure is the key.

22. What if a Christian sees me going into a theater?

There will be some who will object to many of the things you do as you bridge back into the non-Christian world. Don't kick the yapping dogs! If you must choose between a lost soul and a petty Christian, go with the lost soul. If your conscience is clear, you see nothing in Scripture that forbids your plans, and you sense a green light from God, go ahead! Don't try to offend anyone, but respond to biblical priorities. Try to be like Christ!

23. What do I do if my neighbor shows up with some liquor?

Panic. It's inevitable. Tell them to:

a. leave it outside.

b. bring it inside, but leave it in the sack.

c. bring it inside, take it out of the sack, and you'll serve it for them.

d. bring it inside, take it out of the sack, and you'll join them.

Am I saying Christians should drink? *Not at all.* That's not what I'm saying. I'm saying a Christian should do what he/she has the freedom and the inclination to do. That's not for you or me to judge. So obviously, we won't. Right?

24. What about the risk of having non-Christians around my kids?

It's a risk. While your kids may learn new vocabulary words, they also may learn what happens when Christ becomes a reality in a friend's life. They should learn how to interface with the reality of a non-Christian world . . . if you help them do it, that is. Continuing contacts with nonbelievers provide many marvelous, teachable moments. Such unplanned interchange provides a wonderful curriculum for life.

25. When's the best time to start?

That's the easiest question of all. Start right now! Determine *right now* that you will take your place in God's redemptive army. Plan out a strategy appropriate to your own gifts and interests. Look for potential contacts. And pray, Pray, *PRAY!* Effective evangelism begins and ends with God. It's successful only to the degree he's involved. And there's no better way to ensure his involvement than to pray. Right now!